SCHOLASTIC
Spelling™
Louisa Moats and Barbara Foorman

Contents

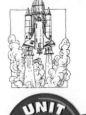

Contents

Contents

Spelling Strategies
Word Study Path

See the word →

See
Look at the letters in the word.

Say
Pronounce the word, and say the letters aloud. Then say the word in syllables.

Link
Break the word into syllables and meaningful parts. Mark the prefixes, suffixes, roots, and endings.

Write
Write the word until it "sticks" in your memory. Say the letters as you write. Use the word in a sentence.

Check
Keep a personal spelling journal. Get in the habit of looking up words you are not sure of.

Write

7

Spelling Words

carefree
courthouse
everybody
everything
forever
grandparent
haircut
nowhere
skyscraper
somebody
something
wherever   *LOOKOUT WORD*
dead end
no one
polka dot
side effect
sign language
sleeping bag
solar system
tape recorder

Review	Challenge
publicly	solar energy
redesigned	wavelength
automobile	

My Words

_____

_____

_____

Compound Words

A See and Say

The Spelling Concept

sky + scraper = skyscraper
solar + system = solar system

A *compound word* is formed by combining two smaller words. Compound words can be one word, such as *skyscraper*, or two words, such as *solar system*.

> When **where** and **ever** get together, they leave one **e** behind.

MEMORY JOGGER

B Link Sounds and Letters

Say each spelling word. Listen for the two words that make up the compound. On a chart like the one below, write each compound word.

Word Sort

One-Word Compounds	Two-Word Compounds

C Write and Check

Use one of the spelling words to answer the riddle below. Then write your own riddle, using one of the spelling words.

_____

_____

_____

_____

RIDDLE
A knapsack is a bag used to carry books or supplies on your back, but a nap sack is a...

sleeping bag

(A) Build Vocabulary: Nouns and Pronouns

A noun is a word that names a person, place, or thing.

grandparent • skyscraper • nowhere • solar system
tape recorder • sleeping bag • side effect

A pronoun is a word that can be used in place of a noun.

somebody • everybody • everything • something • no one

Use the spelling words shown above to select the correct noun or pronoun to match each clue.

1. a pronoun that tells about one thing
2. a person who has a grandchild
3. a pronoun that tells who you are
4. a place that is a tall building
5. a thing you can use for listening to music
6. a pronoun that tells about all people
7. a place that includes one sun and several planets
8. a pronoun that tells that you ate all your food
9. a pronoun that tells who is home when the house is empty
10. a good thing to have on a camping trip
11. a place that is not anywhere
12. an unpleasant thing that can happen after medicine is taken

(B) Word Study: Compound Words

Look at the underlined word in each compound below. Write the spelling word or words that also contain the underlined word.

13. <u>court</u>room
14. <u>dead</u> letter
15./16. what<u>ever</u>
17. <u>language</u> arts
18. <u>polka</u> band
19. <u>hair</u> clip
20. <u>care</u>worn

Spell Chat
See how many **compound words** you and a classmate can make that include these smaller words: *sun, out, down, under, wind.*

Be a Spelling Sleuth
Look for compound words such as *grandparent* and *skyscraper* on greeting cards, on postcards, and in advertisements.

Spelling Words

carefree	something
courthouse	wherever
everybody	dead end
everything	no one
forever	polka dot
grandparent	side effect
haircut	sign language
nowhere	sleeping bag
skyscraper	solar system
somebody	tape recorder

Review	Challenge
publicly	solar energy
redesigned	wavelength
automobile	

My Words

_____

_____

_____

You may wish to do this activity on a computer.

Spelling Words

carefree	something
courthouse	wherever
everybody	dead end
everything	no one
forever	polka dot
grandparent	side effect
haircut	sign language
nowhere	sleeping bag
skyscraper	solar system
somebody	tape recorder

Review	Challenge
publicly	solar energy
redesigned	wavelength
automobile	

My Words

_____

_____

_____

Quick Write

Use three or four compound words to write a brief description of a TV show or movie you have seen recently.

A Write a Character Sketch

You're a famous Hollywood director, and you want to find an actor who can play a part in your upcoming movie. All the actors you have talked to want to know what the character is like. What are his or her goals? What kind of personality does the character have, and what does he or she look like? Use your imagination and three or four compound words to write a character sketch in which you describe the character in your movie.

B Proofread

Rita made five spelling errors, two capitalization errors, and one punctuation error in her character sketch. Correct them.

Tip

A proper noun names a particular person, place, thing, or idea. Proper nouns are always capitalized.

Jonah: Jonah is a care free, enthusiastic surfer from san diego, California. He is eighteen years old, tall and thin, and to hear him tell it, he has been surfing "forver— since I was ten years old. Now, everybuddy in my family surfs." Jonah is a friendly, helpful person who is always willing to give someone a hand Unlike some people who think surfing is not a career, Jonah doesn't feel it has to be a deadend. He hopes to open a business selling redesined surfboards.

Now proofread your character sketch. Check for spelling, capitalization, and punctuation.

PROOFREADING MARKS

∧ Add

⅄ Add a comma

ꞚꞜ Add quotation marks

⊙ Add a period

ℓ Take out

ᘓ Move

≡ Capital letter

/ Small letter

¶ Indent

A Use the Dictionary:
Alphabetize to the First Letter

Entries in a dictionary are listed in alphabetical order. If a word begins with an *a*, the word will appear near the very beginning of the dictionary. A word starting with an *m* should appear near the middle. One starting with a *u* will appear near the end. Write the spelling word that could appear in your Spelling Dictionary after each of the following words.

cre•a•tive   _____

grand•par•ent   _____

ox•y•gen   _____

sys•tem   _____

vol•ca•noes   _____

B Test Yourself

Add the missing parts of these compound words. Then write the spelling words.

1. tape _ _ _ _ _ _ _ _
2. _ _ _ _ cut
3. for _ _ _ _
4. solar _ _ _ _ _ _
5. _ _ _ _ house
6. every _ _ _ _ _
7. _ _ _ _ end
8. some _ _ _ _
9. _ _ _ _ ever
10. grand _ _ _ _ _ _
11. _ _ _ _ _ dot
12. _ _ _ _ language
13. no _ _ _
14. _ _ _ _ _ body
15. some _ _ _ _ _

16. side _ _ _ _ _ _
17. no _ _ _ _ _
18. _ _ _ _ _ _ _ _ bag
19. _ _ _ _ free
20. sky _ _ _ _ _ _ _

For Tomorrow...
Get ready to share the **compound words** you found. Remember to study for your test!

Get Word Wise

American Sign Language is the language used by most hearing-impaired people in the United States and Canada. Sign language combines hand and body gestures with facial expressions to help people communicate. Most signs stand for words, but some stand for actual letters.

Word Study Strategy

See the word

Say it slowly

Link sounds and letters

Write

Check

END

LESSON 2

Spelling Words

- achieve
- apiece
- brief
- fiery
- interview
- pierce
- preview
- relieve
- skied
- yield
- conceited
- deceitful
- perceive
- protein
- receipt
- receiver
- seize
- veil
- eighty
- foreign *LOOKOUT WORD*

Review	Challenge
wherever	diesel
spaghetti	glacier
beige	

My Words

_____

_____

Words With ie and ei

A See and Say

The Spelling Concept

Long e spelled ie: brief   achieve
Long e spelled ei: protein   seize

The letters *ie* and *ei* can stand for the long e sound. They can also stand for other sounds as in the words fiery, preview, veil, and foreign.

B Link Sounds and Letters

Say each spelling word. Listen for the sound that the letters *ie* or *ei* stand for in each word. Do you hear the long *e* sound, or do the letters stand for another sound? Sort the spelling words on a chart like the one below.

> Here's a rule that rhymes: "**i** before **e** except after c." In eighty, I'd say, **ei** sounds like a.

MEMORY JOGGER

Word Sort

/ē/ spelled with ie	/ē/ spelled with ei	ie or ei stands for another sound

C Write and Check

Here's a riddle to puzzle over. Check your spelling word list for the answer.

Now write a riddle of your own, using another spelling word.

_____

_____

_____

_____

RIDDLE

What asks no question but demands an answer?

a ringing telephone receiver

Ⓐ Build Vocabulary: Base Words

A base word is a word to which a prefix, suffix, or other word ending can be added to form another word.

Prefix + Base Word = New Word   Meaning

pre + view = preview   to view before

Add a prefix, suffix, or other word ending to each word in parentheses to form a spelling word and complete the sentence.

1. (receive) Marcus is the wide ___ for his football team.
2. (deceit) If a politician is ___ , she will not be reelected.
3. (eight) *Around the World in ___ Days* is a famous novel.
4. (view) Marisa had a job ___ today.
5. (conceit) Being confident is different from being ___ .

Ⓑ Word Study: Finding Base Words

Remove one or more prefixes, suffixes, or word endings to find a spelling word in each of the sentences below.

6. Joshua was unyielding and refused to give up.
7. Carla attended the lecture briefly, but she had to leave early.
8. Duane's performance in the school play was an achievement.
9. Anton pierced the bull's-eye with his arrow.
10. Unrelieved stress is not good for your health.
11. The entrance to the tomb went unperceived for centuries.
12. Our community has always welcomed foreigners.
13. A grapefruit is a nonprotein food.
14. Marta unveiled the prizes to the crowd.
15. Elsa previewed the video and enjoyed it.
16. Jorge seized the rail to keep from falling down the steps.

Ⓒ Write

Write three sentences that contain *fiery*, *apiece*, *receipt*, and *skied*.

Be a Spelling Sleuth

You might find words with ie or ei spellings—such as *achieve* and *receiver*—in magazine articles about sports and fitness.
You might also search for words with ie and ei on trading cards or in rules for board games.

Spell Chat

Turn to the person next to you and brainstorm three more words with **ie** and **ei** that have the long *e* sound.

Spelling Words

achieve	conceited
apiece	deceitful
brief	perceive
fiery	protein
interview	receipt
pierce	receiver
preview	seize
relieve	veil
skied	eighty
yield	foreign

Review	Challenge
wherever	diesel
spaghetti	glacier
beige	

My Words

_____

_____

_____

Spelling Words

achieve	conceited
apiece	deceitful
brief	perceive
fiery	protein
interview	receipt
pierce	receiver
preview	seize
relieve	veil
skied	eighty
yield	foreign

Review	Challenge
wherever	diesel
spaghetti	glacier
beige	

My Words

_____

_____

_____

Quick Write

List the highlights of a favorite day trip, museum visit, camping trip, or vacation. Include spelling words like *perceive* and *seize*.

A Write a Narrative

You may wish to do this activity on a computer.

Imagine that you're traveling all the way to California from the Midwest in a stagecoach. The year is 1868. Tell about the problems you would face on your trip. Use your spelling words and at least one compound sentence in your narrative.

B Proofread

Diego wrote a narrative about a problem he faced on his trip out West. He made five spelling errors, two capitalization errors, and one error in a compound sentence. Correct them.

Tip
Two simple sentences can be combined into a compound sentence.

> Until last week, we'd been traveling a well-worn section of the trail. Now, I percieve we've taken off on a shortcut I'm wondering if the trail boss knows what he's doing. It's been three days since we had any protien. I've rationed everyone to two slices of bread a piece, morning and night. I worry that the fellow who sold us the map at fort bridge was deceitfull. I'm thinking maybe we should turn back from whereever we are and retrace our steps.

PROOFREADING MARKS

∧	Add
⊼	Add a comma
⸜⸝	Add quotation marks
⊙	Add a period
ℓ	Take out
↶	Move
≡	Capital letter
/	Small letter
¶	Indent

Now proofread your narrative. Check your spelling, capitalization, and punctuation. Pay close attention to your use of compound sentences.

A Use the Dictionary: Guide Words

Guide words at the top of a dictionary page tell you the first and last entry words that appear on that page. If the word you're looking for falls alphabetically between the guide words, it can be found on that page.

Look at the sample guide words below. Which spelling words in this lesson can be found between each of these guide words?

reason ▶ recipe

_____   _____

B Test Yourself

Fill in the missing letters to make a spelling word.
Then write the complete word.

1. for _ _ gn
2. sk _ _ d
3. prot _ _ n
4. rec _ _ ver
5. _ _ ghty
6. rec _ _ pt
7. s _ _ ze
8. v _ _ l
9. interv _ _ w
10. f _ _ ry
11. br _ _ f
12. rel _ _ ve
13. ach _ _ ve
14. p _ _ rce
15. conc _ _ ted
16. ap _ _ ce

17. prev _ _ w
18. y _ _ ld
19. dec _ _ tful
20. perc _ _ ve

For Tomorrow...

Get ready to share the **ie** and **ei** words that you found. Remember to study for the test!

Get Word Wise

The word *ski* is a variation of the Norwegian word *skid*, which means "a thin strip of wood." Today, people ski for sport and as a means of traveling from place to place across the snow.

Word Study Strategy

See the word

Say it slowly

Link sounds and letters

Write

Check

END

Spelling Words

barbecue
easel
poem
skiing
tongue
autumn
condemn
solemn   *LOOKOUT WORD*
pastime
peninsula
barricade
issue
Mississippi
Massachusetts
Tennessee
tissue
athlete
athletic
hundredth
schedule

Review	Challenge
foreign	buffet
suspense	penicillin
calendar	

My Words

_____
_____
_____

Tricky Words

A See and Say

The Spelling Concept

autumn	silent n
barricade	double r
hundredth	hard-to-hear d
pastime	single t

Some words are tricky because they have silent letters, hard-to-hear letters, or double letters. Other tricky words seem like they should have double letters but don't.

I can set up my easel with ease at the barbecue, if you give me my cue.

MEMORY JOGGER

B Link Sounds and Letters

Say each spelling word. Look for the part of the word that might give you trouble. Then create a chart similar to the one below. Write the word in the column that makes the most sense to you. Some words may appear in more than one column.

Word Sort

Silent Letter	Double Letters	Other Tricky Problems

C Write and Check

Can you figure out this tongue twister? Try doubling or adding silent letters to some of the words. Then use some spelling words to create your own tongue twister.

_____
_____
_____

TONGUE TWISTER
Ten ter_ific talkers from Ten_es_e_ told a tal_.

(Ten terrific talkers from Tennessee told a tale.)

Ⓐ Build Vocabulary: **Antonyms**

Antonyms are a pair of words with opposite meanings. Write the spelling word that is the antonym of each word below.

1. lighthearted   **3.** open

2. forgive   **4.** spring

Ⓑ Word Study: **Content-Area Words**

Sometimes words are connected to the study of certain content areas. Write the spelling word that fits each definition below.

Social Studies

5. the principal river of the United States

6. a state in the southeast United States

7. a state in the northeast United States

8. a piece of land that sticks out from a larger land mass

9. an outdoor meal with food cooked on a grill

10. an enjoyable entertainment

11. a matter of public debate

Science

12. a mass of similar cells

13. a movable mouth muscle used for tasting

Physical Education

14. someone trained in sports or games

15. good at sports

16. traveling on runners over snow or water

Arts

17. folding stand that supports a painting

18. writing that often has rhythm and rhyme

Math

19. a part of something that has been divided into 100 pieces

20. a plan or program

Be a Spelling Sleuth

Look for tricky words in restaurant menus, advertisements, and papers sent home by the principal.

Spell Chat

Ask the person next to you to name three words she or he finds **tricky**. Try to spell the words. Share ideas about how to remember their spellings.

Spelling Words

barbecue	barricade
easel	issue
poem	Mississippi
skiing	Massachusetts
tongue	Tennessee
autumn	tissue
condemn	athlete
solemn	athletic
pastime *LOOKOUT WORD*	hundredth
peninsula	schedule

Review	Challenge
foreign	buffet
suspense	penicillin
calendar	

My Words

_____

_____

_____

Spelling Words

barbecue	barricade
easel	issue
poem	Mississippi
skiing	Massachusetts
tongue	Tennessee
autumn	tissue
condemn	athlete
solemn	athletic
pastime	hundredth
peninsula	schedule

LOOKOUT WORD

Review	Challenge
foreign	buffet
suspense	penicillin
calendar	

My Words

_____
_____
_____
_____

Quick Write

List four characteristics of a place you know. Look over your spelling list for words you might use.

A Write a Biographical Sketch

You may wish to do this activity on a computer.

Write a biographical sketch of your favorite athlete or musical performer. What makes you like this person? Use vivid verbs and descriptive adjectives to make the athlete or musician come to life.

B Proofread

Sarah wrote a biographical sketch about Jim Thorpe. It contains four spelling errors, one punctuation error, and one capitalization error. Correct her errors. Also show where Sarah might have used a semicolon.

Tip
Use a semicolon to link two short sentences.

Jim Thorpe may be the greatest athelete of all time. Thorpe, whose Indian name was Bright Path, was a star in football, baseball, and track. At the 1912 olympics, he kept spectators in suspence as he used his atheletic ability to win gold medals. However, a solemm occasion followed. In 1913, the Amateur Athletic Union withdrew Thorpe's amateur status. His trophies were returned. Twenty years after his death the AAU restored his standing. It was a little late for Bright Path to enjoy his success.

PROOFREADING MARKS

∧ Add
⋀ Add a comma
⌄⌄ Add quotation marks
⊙ Add a period
ℓ Take out
↶↷ Move
≡ Capital letter
/ Small letter
¢ Indent

Now proofread your biographical sketch. Check for spelling, grammar, capitalization, and punctuation.

Ⓐ Use the Dictionary: **Alphabetizing**

Entries in a dictionary are presented in alphabetical order. Once you get to the section for the first letter, you may find hundreds of words beginning with the same letter. You may need to go to the second, third, fourth, or fifth letter of the word to find your entry. Look at this example from the dictionary. The first three letters of each word are the same; the fourth letter determines the alphabetical order.

> **bar • be • cue** /bär bi *ky oo*/ *1. noun* A charcoal grill used for cooking meat and other food outdoors. *2. noun* A meal, usually outdoors, in which food is cooked in this manner. *3. verb* to broil or roast over an open fire.

> **bar • ri • cade** /**bar** ri *kād*/ *1. noun* A barrier to stop people from getting past a certain point *2. verb* to build walls or other obstacles to stop people from reaching someone or something.

If you were looking in a dictionary, between which two of these words would you find *easel*? Between which words would you find *poem*? Show where each word would be found.

ear	pod
ease	poet
east	poetizing
easy	poetry

Ⓑ Test Yourself

Write the spelling words in alphabetical order.

For Tomorrow...
Get ready to share words with **tricky** spellings that you came across. Remember to study for the test!

Get Word Wise

Peninsula comes from the Latin words *paene*, which means "almost," and *insula*, which means "island." A peninsula is indeed almost an island. Except on one side, it is surrounded by water.

Word Study Strategy

See the word

Say it slowly

Link sounds and letters

Write

Check

END

LESSON 4

Spelling Words

- civilize
- civilization
- authorize
- authorization
- fascinate
- fascination
- donate
- donation
- appreciate *(LOOKOUT WORD)*
- appreciation
- hibernate
- hibernation
- reserve
- reservation
- conserve
- conservation
- relax
- relaxation
- present
- presentation

Review	Challenge
pastime	punctuation
prescription	demonstration
commotion	

penicillin
suspense

Suffixes -ation and -ion

A See and Say

The Spelling Concept

Verb	+	Suffix	(–) Minus Silent e	=	Noun
civilize		-ation	e		civilization
donate		-ion	e		donation

Many verbs can be changed to nouns by adding the suffix -ation or -ion. In most cases, -ation or -ion is added to a verb after the silent e is dropped.

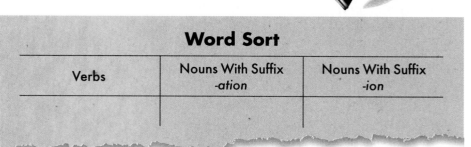

Eat the **e** in appreciat**e** and you'll have my appreciat**ion**.

MEMORY JOGGER

B Link Sounds and Letters

Say each spelling word. Listen for the -ation or -ion at the end of the noun form of each verb. Then sort the spelling words on a chart like the one below.

Word Sort

Verbs	Nouns With Suffix -ation	Nouns With Suffix -ion

C Write and Check

Here are word puzzles to puzzle over.

1. Think of a five-letter word for "to rest." _ _ _ _ _
   Stretch it out into "a period of rest." _ _ _ _ _ _ _ _ _ _

2. Think of a six-letter word for "to give something as a present." _ _ _ _ _ _
   Stretch it out to mean "the actual gift." _ _ _ _ _ _ _ _

Use some spelling words to write your own word puzzle.

_____

_____

Ⓐ Build Vocabulary: Word Meanings

Read the word clues below. Write the spelling word that has a meaning similar to each clue.

1. to improve someone's manners
2. to attract and hold someone's attention
3. to enjoy and understand
4. to give a gift in a formal way
5. to save something from loss or waste
6. to rest and take things easy
7. to give official permission
8. to spend the winter sleeping
9. to give as a present; contribute
10. to save or set aside

Ⓑ Word Study: Adding Suffixes

The suffixes -ation and -ion can mean "the act of" or "the condition of being." Add -ation or -ion to each verb in parentheses to form a noun that completes the sentence.

11. (civilize) We studied an ancient _____ in history class.
12. (appreciate) I sent you a thank-you note to show my _____.
13. (fascinate) The story of Sitting Bull fills me with _____.
14. (present) The TV channel had a special _____ on dolphins.
15. (conserve) Water _____ can help in times of drought.
16. (relaxed) Saturday is a day of _____ for some people.
17. (authorize) You need a written _____ to visit Cape Kennedy.
18. (hibernate) Do bears wake up during their _____?
19. (donate) Mrs. Liu gave a _____ to the school.
20. (reserve) We made a dinner _____.

Spell Chat
Challenge the person next to you to name the past-tense form of each verb on the spelling list.

Be a Spelling Sleuth
Look for words that end with the suffix -ation, such as *civilization* and *presentation*, in newspaper or magazine articles on current events or science topics.

Spelling Words

civilize	hibernate
civilization	hibernation
authorize	reserve
authorization	reservation
fascinate	conserve
fascination	conservation
donate	relax
donation	relaxation
appreciate ᴸᴼᴼᴷᴼᵁᵀ ᵂᴼᴿᴰ	present
appreciation	presentation

Review	Challenge
pastime	punctuation
prescription	demonstration
commotion	

My Words

_____
_____
_____

You may wish to do this activity on a computer.

Spelling Words

civilize	hibernate
civilization	hibernation
authorize	reserve
authorization	reservation
fascinate	conserve
fascination	conservation
donate	relax
donation	relaxation
appreciate LOOKOUT WORD	present
appreciation	presentation

Review	Challenge
pastime	punctuation
prescription	demonstration
commotion	

My Words

_____

_____

_____

Quick Write

Write a flashback about one of your favorite memories. Use as many spelling words as you can.

A Write a Nonfiction Narrative

What exciting thing have you done lately? It might have been a trip you took, or a game you were part of. Write two narrative paragraphs about your experience. Include at least four spelling words and at least one proper noun.

B Proofread

Read Sanchia's nonfiction narrative that describes an exciting trip she took with her uncle. It has four spelling errors, one capitalization error, and two punctuation errors. Correct them.

Tip
A declarative sentence always ends with a period.

> I love to spend time with my Uncle Julio He likes to do things on the spur of the moment. One day he called my mother and invited us to go camping. His invitation had come at just the right time. "We're going far away from civilizashun," he said. "we'll be able to rilax and apprechiate the beauty of nature."
>
> When we arrived at the lake, Uncle Julio jumped out of the car and made a big comotion. Look, Sanchia!" he said. "Wild berries! These will make a great snack!" His excitement is one reason I love being with my uncle.

PROOFREADING MARKS

∧	Add
⋏	Add a comma
⌄⌄	Add quotation marks
⊙	Add a period
ℓ	Take out
⌒	Move
≡	Capital letter
/	Small letter
¢	Indent

Now proofread your narrative aloud. Listen and check for errors in spelling, punctuation, and capitalization.

A Use the Dictionary: Parts of Speech

Study the dictionary entry below for the word *authorize*. Notice the label that shows the part of speech. *Authorize* is a verb. At the end of the dictionary entry, other related forms of the word are presented in dark type.

> **au•thor•ize** /ô thə *rīz*/ **verb** To give official permission for something to happen. ▷ **authorizing, authorized**

Look up the word *authorization* in your Spelling Dictionary. What part of speech is *authorization*? Write your own sentences, using both these spelling words.

B Test Yourself

Complete the spelling equations to find a spelling word. Write each word.

1. hibernated - ed + ion =
2. uncivilize - un - e + ation =
3. presentation - ation =
4. unreserve - un =
5. fascinates - s =
6. civilizing - ing + e =
7. appreciate - e + ion =
8. donations - s =
9. hibernating - ing + e =
10. donated - ed + e =
11. conserving - ing + ation =
12. fascinate - e + ion =
13. preauthorize - pre - e + ation =
14. unrelaxed - un -ed =
15. conserving - ing + e =
16. unappreciated - un - ed + e =
17. unreservedly - un - edly + ation =
18. relaxed - ed + ation =
19. authorizing - ing + ation =
20. presented - ed + ation =

For Tomorrow...

Get ready to share the words with the suffixes **-ation** and **-ion** that you found in newspapers and magazines. Remember to study for the test!

Get Word Wise

Civilize and *civilization* come from Latin, the language of ancient Rome. In Latin, *civis* means "citizen," and *civilis* means "relating to a citizen; polite." What do you think the Roman attitude was toward citizenship?

Word Study Strategy

See the word

Say it slowly

Link sounds and letters

Write

Check

END

Spelling Words

audience
audio
audible
auditorium
audition
audiovisual
video *LOOKOUT WORD*
videotape
evident
evidence
provide
vision
visual
visible
visibility
invisible
provision
revise
revision
television

Review	Challenge
appreciate	vista
autobiography	visor
telegraph	

My Words

_____

_____

_____

Words With the Latin Roots aud, vid, vis

A See and Say

The Spelling Concept

Latin Root	Meaning	English Word
aud	to hear	audible
vid	to see	video
vis	act of seeing	visual

Many English words related to hearing and seeing contain the Latin roots *aud* (to hear), *vid* (to see) and *vis* (the act of seeing).

Do you see the e in video?

MEMORY JOGGER

B Link Sounds and Letters

Say each spelling word. Look and listen for the Latin root *aud*, *vid*, or *vis*. Then write each word on a chart similar to the one below.

Word Sort

aud	vid	vis

C Write and Check

Which spelling word do you think is about both sound and pictures? _____

Challenge yourself to write a sentence using as many "hearing" or "seeing" words as possible.

_____

_____

_____

Ⓐ Build Vocabulary: Suffixes

Replace the underlined words in the sentences below with spelling words containing the suffix *-al*, *-ible*, *-ent*, *-ion*, or *-ium*.

1. The actor's <u>tryout for a part</u> takes place on a bare stage.
2. In an audition, an actor shows <u>proof</u> of her acting skill.
3. He stands alone on stage, with no props or <u>graphic</u> aids.
4. She must make her voice <u>heard</u> throughout the theater.
5. Her character must be understood by <u>those who watch</u>.
6. Her acting ability is soon <u>obvious</u> to the judges.
7. Plays are often presented in an <u>especially large public room</u>.
8. On radio, actors are invisible, but on stage, they're <u>on view</u>.
9. Actors bring a playwright's <u>imaginary idea</u> to life.

Ⓑ Word Study: Prefixes

Use the meanings of the prefixes to help you to match the spelling words to the definitions below.

re- means "again"
in- means "not"
pro- means "before" or "in advance"

10. to look again and change something
11. to look ahead and prepare for
12. the act of looking again and changing it
13. not able to be seen
14. an action taken to prepare for something

Spell Chat

With a classmate, come up with two new words by adding other prefixes or suffixes to the Latin roots **aud, vid,** or **vis.**

Ⓒ Write

Write sentences that contain the spelling words *audio, video, audiovisual, television, videotape,* and *visibility.* Your sentences could be about a televised weather report.

_____

_____

Be a Spelling Sleuth

The Latin roots aud, vid, and vis often appear in names of electronic equipment and companies dealing with sound and sight. Look in ads for high-tech equipment to find examples of words with the roots aud, vid, and vis.

Spelling Words

audience	provide
audio	vision
audible	visual
auditorium	visible
audition	visibility
audiovisual	invisible
video	provision
videotape	revise
evident	revision
evidence	television

Review	Challenge
appreciate	vista
autobiography	visor
telegraph	

My Words

_____

_____

_____

Spelling Words

audience	provide
audio	vision
audible	visual
auditorium	visible
audition	visibility
audiovisual	invisible
video	provision
videotape	revise
evident	revision
evidence	television

Review	Challenge
appreciate	vista
autobiography	visor
telegraph	

My Words

_____

_____

_____

Quick Write

Write a two-line travel ad for a national park. Use alliteration to make the ad catchy and memorable. Use some spelling words.

Ⓐ Write an Alliterative Poem

You may wish to do this activity on a computer.

Write a four-line poem that uses alliteration. Alliteration is the repeated use of the same sound at the beginning of a group of words. Include a few spelling words in your poem.

Ⓑ Proofread

Read this silly alliterative poem that Jason wrote. It has four spelling errors, one punctuation error, one capitalization error, and a grammar error in which the wrong pronoun form is used. Correct all seven errors.

It was evident vicky didn't apprechiate
Victor's vidotape about an
    invisabel ape.
She said, "A vizible ape would be
    more amusing."
To she, the story seemed very
    confusing?

Tip

If a pronoun is the object of a preposition (to, for), it is always an object pronoun (her, it, them).

Now proofread your poem aloud. Listen and check for errors in spelling, punctuation, capitalization, and grammar. Did you use the correct pronoun for the object of a preposition?

PROOFREADING MARKS

∧ Add

⋏ Add a comma

✎ Add quotation marks

⊙ Add a period

ℓ Take out

↶ Move

≡ Capital letter

/ Small letter

¢ Indent

Ⓐ Use the Dictionary: Entry Words

Dictionaries don't define every form of a word in a separate entry. In the dictionary entry below, notice that additional forms, including the noun *revision*, are listed at the end without definitions. From the definitions given, you can figure out that the noun form must mean "something brought up-to-date or changed."

re·vise /ri vīz/ *verb*

1. To look over again and change or correct; to update. *The new city guide has been thoroughly revised.* **2.** To change or make different. *He'll revise his opinion when he gets the facts.* ▷ *verb* **revising, revised**
▷ *noun* **revision**

Write three sentences, using the three additional forms of *revise* in the dictionary entry above: *revising, revised, revision.*

Ⓑ Test Yourself

Figure out the missing letters. Then write each spelling word.

1. crowded _ _ _ itorium
2. _ _ _ eotape your story
3. the _ _ _ io _ _ _ ual room
4. a tele _ _ _ ion set
5. clear _ _ _ ibility
6. the theater _ _ _ ience
7. re _ _ _ _ the plan
8. 20/20 _ _ _ ion
9. in _ _ _ ible germs
10. _ _ _ io on the radio
11. pro _ _ _ e the food
12. _ _ _ ible voice
13. at the _ _ _ ition
14. e _ _ _ ence of fingerprints
15. re _ _ _ ion of the report
16. pro _ _ _ ion for the future
17. rent a _ _ _ eo
18. _ _ _ ual aid
19. _ _ _ ible difference
20. e _ _ _ ent joy

For Tomorrow...
Bring your own list of words with the Latin roots **aud, vid,** and **vis** to share with the class. Remember to study for your test!

Get Word Wise

With the invention of the movies in the 1900s, a new word was coined from ancient Latin roots—audiovisual. Teachers soon saw how audiovisual technology could help students learn. Students soon saw it was fun.

Word Study Strategy

See the word

Say it slowly

Link sounds and letters

Write

Check

END

NATIVE AMERICAN FOLKTALE

Write words from the box to complete the story.

perceive	invisible	deceitful
evidence	present	vision

There once was a handsome and powerful young warrior named Strong Wind. He had the power to hide himself from the __(1)__ of others. All the young maidens wanted to marry him, so he had to think up a plan to help him __(2)__ which one should be his wife. Every evening Strong Wind would __(3)__ himself to his sister, but he would be __(4)__ to the maiden who wanted to win him. The sister would ask, "Do you see him?" The maiden would say "Yes." Then the sister would ask, "What does he use for a bow? What is his sled made of?" The maiden would guess, and her answer would be __(5)__ that she had been __(6)__ and lied.

everybody	conceited	appreciate	everything

In the same village lived a young maiden and her two older sisters. The young maiden's beauty and gentleness was something her sisters did not __(7)__ . They treated her cruelly and made her do __(8)__ around the house. Both older sisters were __(9)__ and thought they could win Strong Wind. Like __(10)__ else, they failed.

appreciation	provide	visible
evident	solemn	no one

The young maiden wanted a chance to win Strong Wind, and his sister was glad to __(11)__ it. When Strong Wind approached, his sister asked, "Do you see him?" The girl saw __(12)__ and said so. It was __(13)__ that the girl was truthful, and Strong Wind had a great __(14)__ for truthfulness. His sister asked again in a __(15)__ voice, "Do you see him?" This time the maiden said, "Yes, his bow is the rainbow and his sled is all the stars in the Milky Way." Then the sister understood that Strong Wind had made himself __(16)__ to the maiden and had chosen her to be his wife.

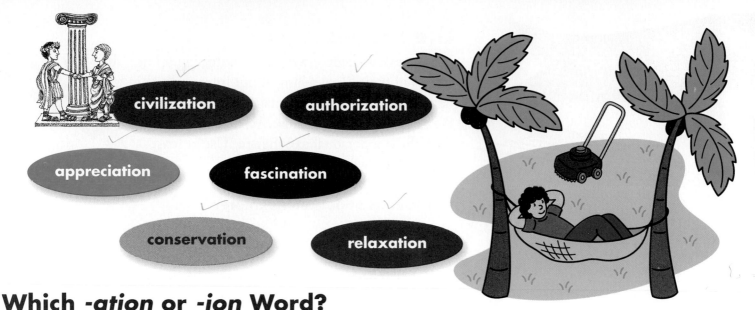

civilization

authorization

appreciation

fascination

conservation

relaxation

Which *-ation* or *-ion* Word?

Write the Review Word ending with *-ation* or *-ion* that fits each of these word clues.

1. people and culture

2. intense interest

3. taking it easy

4. valuing someone or something

5. being careful and not wasteful

6. official approval

What Do You Do If...

Write the Review Word that tells what you do in these situations.

| achieve | audition | condemn | seize |
| donate | yield | preview | |

7. You want a part in a musical?

8. You want to see if a movie is worth viewing?

9. You want to help others?

10. You want to let another car go first?

11. You want to grab something quickly?

12. You disapprove of something?

13. You want to reach a goal?

TRY THIS

Match words from each column to create a spelling word. Then write the whole word.

1. care   a. scraper
2. every   b. cut
3. sky   c. free
4. hair   d. house
5. court   e. body

1. _____

2. _____

3. _____

4. _____

5. _____

sign language
videotape
audible
peninsula
schedule
interview
audience
athlete
presentation
skied
skiing
something
foreign
athletic

Tip

If you're not sure if a compound word is one or two words, check the dictionary.

Life Stories

Many famous people write their autobiographies, the stories of their lives, telling about interesting things that have happened to them. Imagine that you are each of the people described below. Write two sentences describing a personal experience. Use at least two spelling words in each sentence.

A famous underwater explorer

_____

_____

_____

_____

A superstar's bodyguard

_____

_____

_____

_____

A world-champion skier

_____

_____

_____

_____

Look back at the words you misspelled on your Unit 1 Posttests. Use them to write about more experiences.

Tell About It

Choose one of the experiences you wrote about, and expand upon it. Proofread your work for spelling, capitalization, grammar, and punctuation.

PROOFREADING MARKS

∧	Add
⊼	Add a comma
⌄⌄	Add quotation marks
⊙	Add a period
ℓ	Take out
⌒	Move
≡	Capital letter
/	Small letter
¢	Indent

Write It Right

Imagine this. You write a book that gets published, but when you see the first copy of your book, you notice there's a spelling error in the title! Pretty embarrassing, right? Write eight book titles. Use the spelling words listed. Check to make sure there are no spelling errors.

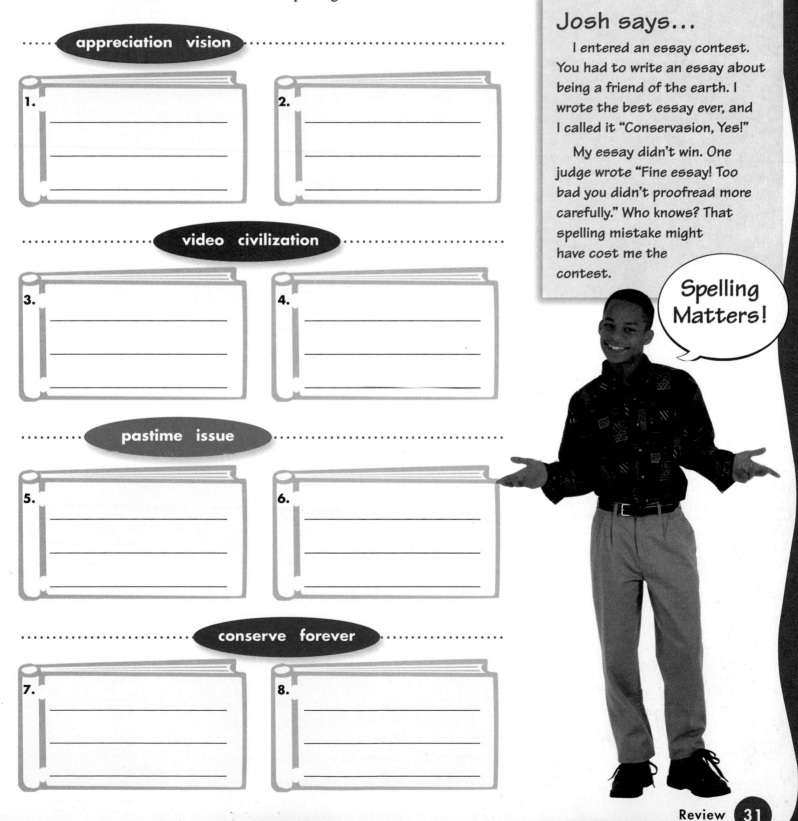

appreciation   vision

1. _____

2. _____

video   civilization

3. _____

4. _____

pastime   issue

5. _____

6. _____

conserve   forever

7. _____

8. _____

Josh says...

I entered an essay contest. You had to write an essay about being a friend of the earth. I wrote the best essay ever, and I called it "Conservasion, Yes!"

My essay didn't win. One judge wrote "Fine essay! Too bad you didn't proofread more carefully." Who knows? That spelling mistake might have cost me the contest.

Spelling Matters!

Spelling Words

adapt
adopt
advice
advise
council
counsel
desert
dessert *LOOKOUT WORD*
proceed
precede
cereal
serial
disinterested
uninterested
recent
resent
moral
morale
hanger
hangar

Review	Challenge
video	compliment
sense	complement
effect	

My Words

_____
_____
_____

Easily Confused Words

Ⓐ See and Say

The Spelling Concept

Word	Meaning
desert (di **zûrt**)	to abandon someone or something
desert (**dez** ərt)	a dry, often sandy place
dessert (di **zûrt**)	a food usually served at the end of a meal

Many pairs of words in English sound very similar and are spelled a lot alike. These words are often confused.

Ⓑ Link Sounds and Letters

Say each pair of spelling words and listen for any differences in pronunciation. Sort each word pair on a chart like the one below.

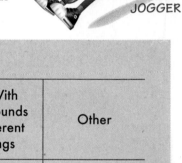

It takes two s's to make dessert because it is so sweet.

MEMORY JOGGER

Word Sort

Pairs With Different Vowel Sounds	Pairs With Different Consonant Sounds	Pairs With Same Sounds but Different Spellings	Other

Ⓒ Write and Check

Complete this funny sentence below with two spelling words.

If you _____ Jim in the _____,
he won't be home in time for _____.

Write your own funny sentence expressing the different meanings of two easily confused spelling words.

_____

_____

A Build Vocabulary: Synonyms

Synonyms are words that have the same meaning or nearly the same meaning. Write the spelling words that are synonyms for the clues below.

1. suggestions
2. honest
3. accept
4. continue
5. sweets
6. dislike
7. garage
8. introduce
9. impartial
10. grain
11. group

12. new
13. recommend
14. indifferent

Spell Chat
Challenge the person next to you to think of two suffixes that could be added to the spelling words. Examples: *recently, adopted.*

B Word Study: Suffixes

The suffixes -*er* and -*or* mean "one who." In each sentence below, -*er* or -*or* has been added to a spelling word. Write the spelling word that relates to the underlined word.

15. I like the <u>counselor</u> who runs my group at camp.
16. The <u>deserter</u> was sorry he ran away from battle.
17. The <u>adapter</u> wrote a screenplay based on a novel.

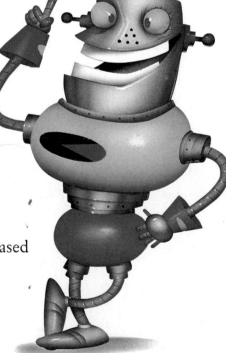

C Write

Write three questions, using the words *hanger, morale,* and *serial.*

_____

_____

_____

Spelling Words

adapt	cereal
adopt	serial
advice	disinterested
advise	uninterested
council	recent
counsel	resent
desert	moral
dessert 	morale
proceed	hanger
precede	hangar

Review	Challenge
video	compliment
sense	complement
effect	

My Words

_____

_____

_____

You may wish to do this activity on a computer.

Spelling Words

adapt	cereal
adopt	serial
advice	disinterested
advise	uninterested
council	recent
counsel	resent
desert	moral
dessert	morale
proceed	hanger
precede	hangar

dessert — LOOKOUT WORD

Review	Challenge
video	compliment
sense	complement
effect	

My Words

_____

_____

_____

Quick Write

Think about a letter you'd like to write to the editor of a newspaper or a magazine. List points you'd like to make. Use several spelling words.

A Write a Persuasive Letter

Get ready to go on an archaeological dig in Egypt! Before you leave, write a letter to persuade a friend to join you. Brainstorm a list of easily confused words to use in your writing.

B Proofread

Correct this part of Tai's letter. She made five spelling errors, two punctuation errors, and one grammar error.

Tip
Remember that two negatives can't be used to express the same negative idea.

I am convinced that on the shimmering sands of the Egyptian dessert I will find the lost tomb of King Amenhotep IV. I can't think of nothing more exciting than having you help me unlock it's secrets, I advice you to precede immediately to Egypt to help me look for this fascinating relic. Together we will see to it that a vidio is made to record this amazing discovery. I can think of no resent find as exciting as this one.

Now proofread the persuasive paragraph you wrote. Check for correct spelling, punctuation, grammar, and capitalization.

PROOFREADING MARKS

∧	Add
⩘	Add a comma
ⱽⱽ	Add quotation marks
⊙	Add a period
ℓ	Take out
⟳∧	Move
≡	Capital letter
/	Small letter
¶	Indent

Ⓐ Use the Dictionary: Example Sentences

Example sentences can be helpful when you're trying to figure out the difference between easily confused words. In the dictionary entries below, the example sentences are in italics.

---

ad•vice /ad vīs/ *noun* A suggestion about what someone should do. *Grace gave me good advice on how to fix my bike.*

---

ad•vise /ad vīz/ *verb* To give someone information or suggestions. *Tom advised me to stay at home until rush hour was over.* ▷ *verb* advising, advised ▷ *noun* adviser, advisor ▷ *adjective* advisory

---

Write example sentences to clarify the meaning of *desert* and *dessert*.

_____

Ⓑ Test Yourself

Complete each sentence with easily confused spelling-word pairs.

1–2. I ate a delicious, filling ___1___ at an oasis in the ___2___.

3–4. Do you ___3___ me to ask for someone else's ___4___?

5–6. The lawyer served as ___5___ to the security ___6___.

7–8. Shall we ___7___ the old rules or ___8___ new ones?

9–10. Just as Sunday will always ___9___ Monday, my dog will ___10___ to chase a cat if given a chance.

11–12. In the ___11___ *The Adventures of Jerry*, Jerry eats a new box of ___12___ every week.

13–14. Peter will probably give a ___13___ opinion because he is ___14___ in politics.

15–16. We deeply ___15___ the ___16___ insults we just heard.

17–18. ___17___ leaders will lift the ___18___ of their followers.

19–20. The pilot left her jacket on a ___19___ in the airplane ___20___.

For Tomorrow...

Be ready to share all the spelling words you collected. Remember to study for your test.

Get Word Wise

Say *cereal* and most people think of a box of dry flakes. Yet, the word refers to all grains, the plants that produce them, and the foods made from them. *Cereal* comes from the Latin *Ceres*, the Roman goddess of farming.

Word Study Strategy

See the word

Say it slowly

Link sounds and letters

Write

Check

END

Spelling Words

duct
conduct *(LOOKOUT WORD)*
conductor
deduction
educate
educator
education
reduce
reduction
produce
production
product
productive
introduce
introduction
introductory
introducing
conducting
reducing
producing

Review	Challenge
dessert	aqueduct
nowhere	productivity
promote	

My Words

_____

_____

_____

Words With the Latin Root duc

Ⓐ See and Say

The Spelling Concept

duct	a pipe or tube that leads from one place to another
introduce	to bring forth for the first time; to present
educate	to lead to knowledge; to teach

Many English words contain the Latin root *duc*, which means "lead" or "bring forth." The root can be spelled *duc*, *duct*, or *duce*.

The conductor was very productive and conducted throughout the whole production.

MEMORY JOGGER

Ⓑ Link Sounds and Letters

Say each spelling word. Listen for the Latin root *duc*. Then look for the way the root is spelled. Sort the spelling words on a chart like this one.

Word Sort

Root Only	Prefix + Root	Prefix + Root + Suffix

Ⓒ Write and Check

Write the answers to the word puzzle.

1. What word with the root *duc* explains why you go to school? _ _ _ _ _ _ _ _ _

2. What word do you get if you take away *-ion* and add a suffix meaning "one who"? _ _ _ _ _ _ _ _

3. Take away the last suffix and add the ending *-e* to get _ _ _ _ _ _ _ .

Use some spelling words to write your own word puzzle.

_____

A Build Vocabulary: Roots

All of the following definitions relate to the meaning of the Latin root *duc*, "to lead or bring forth." Write a spelling word for each definition.

1. pipe or tube
2. behavior
3. orchestra leader
4. to teach someone
5. teacher
6. knowledge and skills that a person learns
7. to make smaller
8. the act of making something smaller
9. to bring in something new
10. the act of bringing in something new
11. serving to introduce something
12. something that is manufactured
13. producing good results

Spell Chat

Start a sentence with one spelling word, and ask a person next to you to continue the sentence with another spelling word. Try this a few times.

B Word Study: Related Forms

Knowing the Latin root of a word can help you identify and spell other words that are related to it. What spelling words can you add to each group of words below?

deduct, deductive, ___14___

reduce, reduction, ___15___

introduce, introduction, introductory, ___16___

conductor, conduct, ___17___

C Write

Write an original tongue twister, using the spelling words *producing*, *produce*, and *production*.

_____

_____

_____

Be a Spelling Sleuth

Look in newspapers for words with the Latin root duc. You can find words like *educate* and *education*. Make a list of the words you find.

Spelling Words

duct	production
conduct	product
conductor	productive
deduction	introduce
educate	introduction
educator	introductory
education	introducing
reduce	conducting
reduction	reducing
produce	producing

Review	Challenge
dessert	aqueduct
nowhere	productivity
promote	

My Words

_____

_____

_____

Spelling Words

duct	production
conduct *(LOOKOUT WORD)*	product
conductor	productive
deduction	introduce
educate	introduction
educator	introductory
education	introducing
reduce	conducting
reduction	reducing
produce	producing

Review	Challenge
dessert	aqueduct
nowhere	productivity
promote	

My Words

_____

_____

_____

Quick Write

Use as many words with the Latin root **duc** as you can to write an advertisement for one of the robots from the Metalbody Factory Outlet.

A Write an Article

You may wish to do this activity on a computer.

A factory that manufactures robots has just opened in your area. Write a brief article for your local paper announcing a guided tour of the factory. Brainstorm a list of words with the Latin root *duc* that you might use.

B Proofread

Below is Clay's news article. It has four spelling errors, two capitalization errors, and two punctuation errors. Correct them.

Tip
Commas should be used to separate three or more items in a series.

> Have you ever seen a robot that looks like a reperdution of a human being There are several at the new Metalbody Factory Outlet on Computer street. For a fascinating introdoction to robotics, take the factory's guided tour this saturday at noon. Tour condukter Robbie Metalbody wants to promotte the factory's products and educate visitors about robots for the home school, or office. You can look forward to increasing your knowledge and education in the science of robotics.

PROOFREADING MARKS

∧ Add

⅄ Add a comma

∨∨ Add quotation marks

⊙ Add a period

ℓ Take out

↶↷ Move

≡ Capital letter

/ Small letter

¶ Indent

Now proofread your article. Check for correct spelling, grammar, capitalization, and punctuation, including the correct use of commas.

A Use the Dictionary: Definitions

When an entry word has more than one meaning, the different definitions are usually numbered. Read the definitions of *conduct* from the Spelling Dictionary:

con·duct

1. /kən dukt/ *verb* To organize and carry out. *The police will conduct an inquiry into the crime.* **2.** /kən dukt/ *verb* To direct musicians. **3.** /kon dukt/ *noun* Behavior.

Which meaning of *conduct* appears in each of these sentences? Write the number.

- The soldier won a medal for good conduct. _____
- Who will conduct the band after Mrs. Kim retires? _____
- The doctors will conduct a new study of heart disease. _____

Now write your own sentences to illustrate two of the definitions.

B Test Yourself

Fill in the missing letters to make a spelling word. Then write the complete word.

1. _ _ _ t
2. _ _ ducing
3. e _ _ _ ator
4. _ _ duc _
5. c _ _ duc _ _ _ _
6. _ duc _ _ _
7. de _ _ _ tion
8. _ _ _ duc _ _ _
9. _ _ _ duc _
10. ed _ _ _ ti _ _
11. pro _ _ _ in _
12. _ _ _ _ _ duce
13. _ _ _ duct
14. in _ _ _ duc _ _ _
15. intro _ _ _ to _ _
16. p _ o _ _ c _
17. _ _ duc _ _ on
18. p _ _ du _ _ _ _ n
19. _ _ _ ducti _ _
20. in _ _ _ duc _ _ _ _

For Tomorrow...
Be prepared to discuss the places where you found words with *duc*. Remember to study for your test!

Get Word Wise
Do you know a teacher who is a leader? The word *educator* comes from the Latin word *ducere*, which means "to lead." In ancient Rome, teachers were viewed as people who led others out of ignorance.

Word Study Strategy

See the word

Say it slowly

Link sounds and letters

Write

Check

END

Spelling Words

victory
victorious
compete
competition
similar
similarity
theater
theatrical 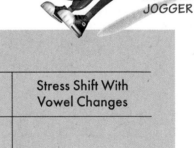 LOOKOUT WORD
poet
poetic
compare
comparison
define
definition
relate
relation
solve
solution
resolve
resolution

Review	Challenge
conduct	democratic
yield	democracy
transportation	

My Words

_____

_____

_____

Learn and Spell

Stress Shift and Vowel Changes

Ⓐ See and Say

The Spelling Concept

Word	Pronunciation	Word + Ending	Pronunciation
victory	**vik** tə rē	victorious	vik **tôr** ē əs
poet	**pō** it	poetic	pō **et** ik

When an ending is added to a word, there may be a stress shift and a change in vowel sound. For example, the first syllable is accented in *victory*. When *-ious* is added to make the word *victorious*, the accent shifts to the second syllable. Notice also that the vowel sound changes. Sometimes there is only a stress shift with no vowel change.

Ⓑ Link Sounds and Letters

Say each pair of related words. Listen for the change in the accented syllable. Then listen to see if a vowel sound also changes. Then sort the words on a chart like the one below.

Remember that **Vic**tor is always **vic**torious.

MEMORY JOGGER

Word Sort

Shorter Word	No Stress Shift	Stress Shift With Vowel Changes

Ⓒ Write and Check

What are the related spelling words that complete each sentence?

1. When you _____ a puzzle, you find a _____.

2. When you _____ to do something, you make a _____.

Now write your own sentence that uses two related words.

_____

A Synonyms

Synonyms are words that have the same or almost the same meaning.
Write the spelling word that is a synonym for each word or phrase.

1. tell
2. likeness
3. auditorium
4. figure out
5. contest
6. outcome
7. triumph
8. family member
9. explain
10. settle
11. meaning
12. answer

Spell Chat
With a classmate, think of ways to remember that there is an *i* in *comparison*.

B Word Study: Adjectives

An adjective is a word that describes a noun. *Happy* and *gigantic* are adjectives. Write the adjective form of each spelling word in parentheses.

13. (victory) a _____ team
14. (similarity) a _____ appearance
15. (theater) a _____ event
16. (poet) a _____ speech

C Write

Write newspaper headlines, using these words: *compete* and *poet*, *compare* and *comparison*.

_____

_____

_____

Be a Spelling Sleuth

Make a list of related words you might encounter at a theater or sporting event. For example, at a show you might see the word *theater*. Later, you might read a review of the *theatrical* event.

Spelling Words

victory	compare
victorious	comparison
compete	define
competition	definition
similar	relate
similarity	relation
theater	solve
theatrical	solution
poet	resolve
poetic	resolution

LOOKOUT WORD

Review	Challenge
conduct	democratic
yield	democracy
transportation	

My Words

_____

_____

_____

Spelling Words

victory	compare
victorious	comparison
compete	define
competition	definition
similar	relate
similarity	relation
theater	solve
theatrical	solution
poet	resolve
poetic	resolution

Review	Challenge
conduct	democratic
yield	democracy
transportation	

My Words

_____

_____

_____

Quick Write

Jot down your ideas about something you would like to do in a talent show. Use at least three spelling words.

A Write an Informative Paragraph

You may wish to do this activity on a computer.

Your school is having a student talent show. Write a short paragraph in which you provide your community with information about the show. Include at least three of your spelling words.

B Proofread

Jana's paragraph contains six spelling errors, three capitalization errors, and one punctuation error. Correct the errors.

Tip

All nouns that name a specific person, place, or thing are capitalized.

A student Talent Show will be held outside at the children's theater on Starstruck drive. This year's compatition begins at noon on Saturday, September 29. Please arrange your own transpurtation. Performers will compeet in categories similer to those of last year's show. These categories include dancing, singing and acting. Prizes will be awarded to the top performers in each category. You may be victoryous! There will be a victorie party following the awards.

PROOFREADING MARKS

∧	Add
⩓	Add a comma
❝ ❞	Add quotation marks
⊙	Add a period
ℓ	Take out
○∧	Move
≡	Capital letter
/	Small letter
¢	Indent

Now proofread your informative paragraph. Check for correct spelling, capitalization, and punctuation.

Ⓐ Use the Dictionary: Multiple Meanings

Many dictionary entries have more than one definition. Look at the dictionary entry below, for example. It presents two quite different definitions of the word *solution*.

so•lu•tion /sə loo shən/ *noun*

1. The answer to a problem; an explanation. **2.** A mixture formed by dissolving a substance in a liquid.

Write an example sentence for each definition of the word *solution*.

_____

_____

Ⓑ Test Yourself

Complete each spelling word with its missing vowels.

1. v __ ct __ r __
2. c __ mp __ t __ t __ __ __ n
3. s __ m __ l __ r __ t __
4. p __ __ t __ c
5. d __ f __ n __ t __ __ n
6. v __ ct __ r __ __ __ __ s
7. r __ s __ l __ t __ __ n
8. r __ l __ t __
9. s __ lv __
10. th __ __ tr __ c __ l
11. c __ mp __ r __ s __ n
12. th __ __ t __ r
13. s __ m __ l __ r
14. s __ l __ t __ __ n

15. r __ l __ t __ __ n
16. d __ f __ n __
17. c __ mp __ r __
18. c __ mp __ t __
19. r __ s __ lv __
20. p __ __ t

For Tomorrow…

Be ready to share the spelling words you collected. Remember to study for your test!

Get Word Wise

You probably have never thought of poets as "makers," but the word *poet* comes from the Greek word *poietes*, meaning "maker." What do poets make? They make verses that sometimes make us laugh and sometimes make us think.

Word Study Strategy

See the word

Say it slowly

Link sounds and letters

Write

Check

END

LESSON 10

Spelling Words

admit
admitting
admission
admittance
omit
omitting
permit
permitting
permission
dismiss
dismissal
mission
missile *LOOKOUT WORD*
commit
commitment
committee
submit
transmit
transmission
intermission

Review	Challenge
theatrical	noncommittal
peninsula	intermittent
disappearance	

My Words

_____

_____

_____

Words Using mis and mit

A See and Say

The Spelling Concept

dismiss	to send away
transmit	to send from one person or place to another
admitting	allowing someone to enter

Many English words contain the Latin root *mis* or *mit*, which means "to send." The root *mis* is often spelled *miss*.

The *t* in the root *mit* is doubled when it appears in a stressed syllable followed by a vowel.

It takes two m's, two t's, and two e's to form a committee.

MEMORY JOGGER

B Link Sounds and Letters

Say each spelling word. Listen for the Latin roots *mis* and *mit*. Then look at each word to see where the root is located. Sort your spelling words on a chart like this one.

Word Sort

mit plus prefix	*mit* plus prefix and suffix, or other word endings	*mis* plus prefix	*mis* plus suffix	*mis* plus prefix and suffix, or other word endings

C Write and Check

Complete this tongue twister. Which related spelling words go in the blanks?

Doctor Dismus didn't _ _ _ _ _ _ _ us until he heard the
_ _ _ _ _ _ _ _ _ bell.

Now write your own tongue twister. Use at least two of the spelling words.

_____

_____

A Build Vocabulary: Word Parts

Complete each spelling word by providing the correct form of the root *mis* or *mit*. Then write the whole word.

1. ad _ _ _ _ ance
2. ad _ _ _ _ ion
3. per _ _ _ _ ion
4. dis _ _ _ _ al
5. _ _ _ _ ion
6. sub _ _ _

7. _ _ _ _ ile
8. com _ _ _ ment
9. com _ _ _ _ ee
10. trans _ _ _ _ ion
11. inter _ _ _ ion

Be a Spelling Sleuth

Look in science stories and articles about space missions for words with mis and mit. Make a list of the words you find.

B Word Study: Action Verbs

Some of the spelling words are verbs that express action. Read each sentence and write the word that best completes it.

12. When you make a new list please _____ the names that you have already used.

13. The teacher will _____ the class at noon for lunch.

14. If you _____ yourself to something, you promise to see it through.

15. Two radio stations use this equipment to _____ programs.

16. These tickets will _____ you to the stadium.

17. These new ramps will _____ access for people using wheelchairs.

Spell Chat

Turn to the person next to you and challenge him or her to think of another verb with the Latin root **mis** or **mit**.

C Write

Use the words *admitting*, *permitting*, and *omitting* in a short, funny poem.

_____

_____

Spelling Words

admit	dismissal
admitting	mission
admission	missile LOOKOUT WORD
admittance	commit
omit	commitment
omitting	committee
permit	submit
permitting	transmit
permission	transmission
dismiss	intermission

Review	Challenge
theatrical	noncommittal
peninsula	intermittent
disappearance	

My Words

_____

_____

_____

Spelling Words

admit	dismissal
admitting	mission
admission	missile (LOOKOUT WORD)
admittance	commit
omit	commitment
omitting	committee
permit	submit
permitting	transmit
permission	transmission
dismiss	intermission

Review	Challenge
theatrical	noncommittal
peninsula	intermittent
disappearance	

My Words

_____

_____

_____

Quick Write

Write a short description of your favorite science fiction film or book. Use as many words with mit and mis as you can.

A Write a Press Release

You may wish to do this activity on a computer.

A press release is a news item written for the purpose of giving information and promoting something. Write a brief press release for a new science fiction film. Tell about the film's setting and plot. Remember to use quotation marks if you include a quote from someone, and don't forget to include spelling words!

B Proofread

Here is part of the press release Dominique wrote. She made four spelling errors, two capitalization errors, and two punctuation errors. Correct them.

> **Tip**
> Remember to use quotation marks when you write what one person says to another.

"I just love this film," one viewer told me during intermission, and it sure was worth the price of admision."

Remarks like these can be heard all over the United States, as moviegoers view <u>Mision From Mars</u>, the new theatrecal release from Admit One Films. The movie, which is set in the future, tells the exciting story of a martian missile that strikes antarctica, bearing a message. It reads, "You must permite us to land!

Now proofread your press release. Check your spelling, punctuation, and capitalization.

PROOFREADING MARKS

∧	Add
⌃	Add a comma
⌄⌄	Add quotation marks
⊙	Add a period
ℓ	Take out
⌒	Move
≡	Capital letter
/	Small letter
¶	Indent

A Use the Dictionary: Word Endings

When the spelling of a root changes with the addition of -*ing*, -*ed*, or another common ending, most dictionaries will show you the spelling of the new word. For example, in the entry for the verb *permit* below, the dictionary shows that you must double the *t* before adding -*ing* or -*ed*.

per • mit

1. /pər mit/ *verb* To allow. ▷ **permitting, permitted** 2. /pûr mit/ *noun* A written statement giving permission for something, as in *a driving permit*.

Use the three verb forms of *permit*—*permit*, *permitting*, and *permitted*—in three different sentences.

_____

_____

_____

Then write a sentence using the word *permit* as a noun.

_____

B Test Yourself

Fill in the missing letters to make a spelling word. Then write the whole word.

1. _ _ _ miss
2. _ _ _ mitt _ _
3. _ _ _ _ _ mit
4. _ _ _ mitt _ _ _
5. miss _ _ e
6. _ _ _ miss _ _ _
7. _ _ bmit
8. _ _ mmit
9. _ dmit
10. _ _ mitt _ _ _
11. _ mit
12. i _ _ _ _ miss _ _ _

13. miss _ _ n
14. _ _ _ miss _ _
15. _ _ _ mit
16. _ _ _ mit _ _ _ _
17. t _ _ _ _ miss _ _ _
18. _ mit _ _ _ _
19. _ _ miss _ _ _
20. _ _ mitt _ _ _ _

For Tomorrow...
Be prepared to share the words with **mit** and **mis** you discovered in stories and articles about space missions. Don't forget to study for your test!

Get Word Wise

Today we use the word *mission* to refer to a specific goal or task, such as a space mission. At one time, however, *mission* referred to the group of people performing the task.

Word Study Strategy

See the word
Say it slowly
Link sounds and letters
Write
Check
END

Spelling Words

lynx
syrup
myth
rhyme
rhythm LOOKOUT WORD
system
symbol
cymbal
syllable
cylinder
oxygen
synonym
antonym
physical
physician
symptom
hysterical
pyramid
symphony
sympathy

Review	Challenge
missile	symmetrical
relaxation	asymmetrical
typical	

My Words

_____
_____
_____

Words With y as a Vowel

A See and Say

The Spelling Concept

lynx   system   synonym

Some words use the letter *y* to spell /i/ or another vowel sound. The *y* can appear in words of one or more syllables.

Inside a syllable, a y can be /i/.

MEMORY JOGGER

B Link Sounds and Letters

Say each spelling word. Listen for the number of syllables in each word. Sort the words on a chart like the one below.

Word Sort

One Syllable	Two Syllables	Three Syllables	Four Syllables

C Write and Check

Complete the sentences to find out what went on at the silly symphony.

The _____ player dropped her instrument with a crash. The violinists sighed in _____ and lost the _____ .

What else can go wrong? Use one or two spelling words in another sentence about the silly symphony.

_____
_____
_____

A Build Vocabulary: Analogies

An analogy shows a similarity between pairs of words. Write the spelling word that makes the relationship on the right similar to the relationship on the left.

1. *Link* is to *chain* as _____ is to *word*.
2. *Stomach* is to *food* as *lungs* are to _____.
3. *Letter* is to *a, b, c* as _____ is to *+, *, &*.
4. *Silence* is to *calm* as *outburst* is to _____.
5. *Detective* is to *clue* as *doctor* is to _____.
6. *Same* is to *synonym* as *opposite* is to _____.
7. *Circle* is to *cylinder* as *triangle* is to _____.
8. *Sour* is to *lemon* as *sweet* is to _____.
9. *Sleuth* is to *detective* as _____ is to *doctor*.
10. *Drumming* is to *beat* as *clapping* is to _____.
11. *Zucchini* is to *squash* as _____ is to *cat*.
12. *Mental* is to *brain power* as _____ is to *fitness*.

B Plurals

For each of the following spelling words, write the plural form. Remember that most plurals end in *-s*. Add *-es* to words ending in *x*. Change words ending in *y* to *i* before adding *-es*.

13. rhyme   17. symphony
14. sympathy   18. cymbal
15. system
16. cylinder

C Write

Write a sentence, using these spelling words: *myth, synonym*.

_____

_____

_____

Be a Spelling Sleuth

Look through newspapers or magazines, and collect words with y as a vowel from ads or articles. You might find an advertisement for a physician or a science article on different kinds of crystals.

Spell Chat

With a partner, think of two other words that spell /i/ with **y** and then spell them.

Spelling Words

lynx	oxygen
syrup	synonym
myth	antonym
rhyme	physical
rhythm 	physician
system	symptom
symbol	hysterical
cymbal	pyramid
syllable	symphony
cylinder	sympathy

LOOKOUT WORD

Review	Challenge
missile	symmetrical
relaxation	asymmetrical
typical	

My Words

_____

_____

_____

Spelling Words

lynx	oxygen
syrup	synonym
myth	antonym
rhyme	physical
rhythm (LOOKOUT WORD)	physician
system	symptom
symbol	hysterical
cymbal	pyramid
syllable	symphony
cylinder	sympathy

Review	Challenge
missile	symmetrical
relaxation	asymmetrical
typical	

My Words

_____
_____
_____

Quick Write

Write two sentences about music. They could be about different kinds of rhythms, a symphony, or a musical instrument. Include as many spelling words as you can in your sentences.

A Write a Letter

You may wish to do this activity on a computer.

A well-known music group is coming to town. Write a letter to a friend inviting him or her to join you and your family for the concert.

B Proofread

Geraldo made five spelling errors, two punctuation errors, and one grammar error involving subject-verb agreement. Fix all the errors.

Tip
A verb must agree in number with the subject of the sentence.

Dear Desi

My friend Alma plays the cimbles for a simphony orchestra. She gave us tickets for Friday night, October 2. Would you be interested in going with us. The tipical audience at this kind of concert never gets histerical, but I still think you'll have a good time. The musicians in the rithm section is terrific.

Please let me know if you can come.

Sincerely yours,

Geraldo

Now proofread your letter. Check for correct spelling, punctuation, capitalization, and grammar, including subject-verb agreement.

PROOFREADING MARKS

∧	Add
⋏	Add a comma
∜	Add quotation marks
⊙	Add a period
ℓ	Take out
◠	Move
≡	Capital letter
/	Small letter
¢	Indent

A Use the Dictionary: Homophones

Homophones are words that sound alike but have different meanings and are spelled differently, such as *cymbal* and *symbol*. When you're not certain which of two homophones to use, check their definitions in a dictionary.

cym·bal /sim bəl/ *noun*

A musical instrument made of brass and shaped like a plate. It is played by striking it with a stick or another cymbal. **Cymbal** sounds like **symbol**.

sym·bol /sim bəl/ *noun*

A design or an object that represents something else. *On many maps, a small, green pine tree is the symbol for a forest.* **Symbol** sounds like **cymbal**.

Now write a sentence, using both the words *cymbal* and *symbol*.

_____

_____

B Test Yourself

Figure out the missing letters, and then write each spelling word.

1. l _ _ _
2. m _ _ _
3. s _ _ _ p
4. o _ _ _ _ _
5. r _ _ _ _ m
6. _ _ _ _ _ b l e
7. s _ _ _ _ l
8. _ _ _ _ _ _ e r
9. c _ _ _ _ l
10. s _ _ _ e m
11. r _ _ _ e
12. _ _ _ _ _ _ i a n
13. a _ _ _ _ _ m
14. p h _ _ _ _ _ _
15. s _ n _ _ _ m

16. s _ _ _ _ o m
17. _ _ _ _ _ t h y
18. p _ _ _ _ _ d
19. s _ _ _ _ _ n y
20. h _ _ _ _ _ _ _ a l

For Tomorrow...

Be ready to share the words with **y** from ads and articles that you found in newspapers or magazines. Remember to study for your test!

Word Study Strategy

See the word

Say it slowly

Link sounds and letters

Write

Check

END

AN EVENING ~ at the ~ SYMPHONY

Complete each sentence with a word from the box.

admission	morale	rhythm
commitment	physical	symphony

I nspector Mosley closed her eyes and let the **(1)** of the music soothe her. An evening at the **(2)** had been a good idea. The chance to sit quietly was good for her **(3)** and well worth the price of **(4)** . Working on a case that seemed impossible to solve was taking a **(5)** toll. She was exhausted, but even exhaustion couldn't weaken her **(6)** to the case.

compete	dismiss	solution
deduction	proceed	

She couldn't completely **(7)** work from her thoughts. The case began to **(8)** with the music for her attention. She reviewed every clue and every **(9)** she'd made. Why had all her reasoning led nowhere? Why was there still no **(10)** ? How was she going to **(11)** and catch the criminal?

conductor	cereal	mission
cymbal	intermission	theater

A **(12)** crash brought her attention back to the music. She looked around the **(13)** , trying to keep her mind off the case. That's when she noticed the **(14)** who led the orchestra. Then she caught a glimpse of his face. Up on stage was the man she'd been looking for, the man responsible for the theft of several tons of breakfast **(15)** . She checked the program. It would soon be time for **(16)** . She could make her move then. Slowly, she smiled. She was no longer a woman on a desperate **(17)** ; she was a detective who would solve her case.

Accented Syllables

Music has rhythm, and so do words and language. The stressed syllables in words are like the beat. Sometimes the beat changes when an ending is added to a base word. Write the Review Word that's related to each of these words. Then draw an accent mark to show where the stress is in each word.

similarity

comparison

theatrical

morale

competition

1. compete _____

2. moral _____

3. compare _____

4. similar _____

5. theater _____

Latin Roots

Duc comes from the Latin word *ducere*, which means "to lead." The roots *mis* and *mit* come from the Latin word *mittere*, which means "to send." Write the Review Word that best reflects each of the ideas listed below.

education	permission
reduce	dismissal
conduct	missile	introduction

"Leading" Words

6. lead a group to perform music _____

7. less eating leads you to _____ your waistline

8. something that leads to knowledge _____

9. something that leads into the main part _____

"Sending" Words

10. a kind of note that sends consent _____

11. something sent or fired off towards a target _____

12. the act of sending people away _____

WORD BUILDING

Your mission is to write three or more words that include the word *mission*.

_____

_____

_____

_____

_____

antonym	advise
desert	production
define	precede
dessert	productive
rhyme	rhythm
committee	syllable
compare	similar
educator	symphony
hysterical	synonym
commitment	theater
introductory	theatrical

Tip
Remember that in some words, the letter y acts as a vowel.

What a Production!

You are part of a community group that will be writing, directing, or acting in a play. Write a few sentences that answer the following questions. Use at least two spelling words in each sentence.

1. Where will the play be presented?

_____

_____

2. Where is the setting of the play?

_____

_____

3. What is the play about?

_____

_____

4. What skills should the actors, dancers, set designers, and others in the group have?

_____

_____

5. What qualities are important for people who need to work together?

_____

_____

Look back at the words you misspelled on your Unit 2 Posttests. Use some of them to write about the play.

_____

_____

_____

Persuade Me . . .

Write a persuasive paragraph, encouraging people to come to the play. Proofread your work for spelling, capitalization, grammar, and punctuation.

PROOFREADING MARKS

- ∧ Add
- ⋏ Add a comma
- ⌄⌄ Add quotation marks
- ⊙ Add a period
- ℓ Take out
- ↻ Move
- ≡ Capital letter
- ╱ Small letter
- ¶ Indent

Easily Confused Words

There are many examples of words that sound alike or look alike. Sometimes it's easy to mix them up. See how you do with these easily confused words. Write each one in the sentence that reflects the right meaning.

·················· **symbol   cymbal** ········

1. The _____ crash got everyone's attention.

   Then everyone stood as the flag, the _____ of our country, was carried into the stadium.

········· **precede   proceed** ····················

2. Reading a card should _____ opening a present.

   Then you may _____ to open the present.

················· **morale   moral** ················

3. The _____ of the story was "Determination and effort can carry the day."

   Reading it together boosted everyone's _____.

········ **serial   cereal** ····························

4. The incident in the last episode of the _____ was funny.

   It involved a contest to name a new breakfast _____.

················· **hanger   hangar** ·········

5. Don't go into the airplane's _____.

   That coat is too heavy for that plastic _____.

Sarah says...

Since our school marching band was going to be on television, I e-mailed a message to my sister at college to watch. I told her I'd be playing the symbols. She e-mailed back: How do you plan to play a flag and an American bald eagle? So I e-mailed this message to her: I play cymbals. I don't spell them.

Spelling Matters!

"Star" Words

A See and Say

Spelling Words

stardust
stargazer
starlight
starboard
starry-eyed
starless
star-spangled
starfish *LOOKOUT WORD*
stellar
constellation
aster
asterisk
asteroid
disaster
disastrous
astrodome
astronaut
astronomy
astronomer
astronomical

Review	Challenge
rhythm	astrophysics
visibility	star-studded
lunar	

My Words

_____

_____

_____

The Spelling Concept

star	+ dust	=	stardust
ast	+ er	=	aster
stell	+ ar	=	stellar

Many English words include the base word *star*. Other English words are formed from the Greek and Latin roots for *star*: *ast* (Greek) and *stell* (Latin). You will find the "star" words are often related to the sciences.

B Link Sounds and Letters

Say each spelling word. Listen for the base word *star*, the Greek root *ast*, or the Latin root *stell*. Then write the spelling words in the correct column in a chart like the one below.

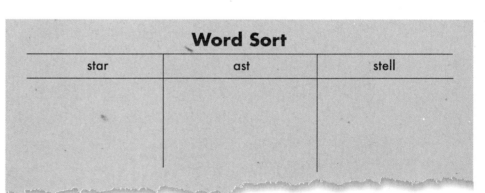

Stellar objects are far, far away.

MEMORY JOGGER

Word Sort		
star	ast	stell

C Write and Check

Use a "star" word to answer the riddle below. Then make up your own riddle, using one of the spelling words. Share your riddle with a classmate.

_____

_____

_____

RIDDLE

What would you call a person who stares at famous people?

a stargazer

A Build Vocabulary: Word Meanings

Do a star search! Write the spelling word that matches each definition.

1. star-shaped mark used in writing
2. scientist who studies stars, planets, and space
3. having to do with space study; enormous
4. space traveler
5. event causing great harm
6. very harmful
7. very small planet-like mass that travels around the sun
8. scientific study of stars
9. without stars
10. a flower with round yellow center
11. the right side of a ship or aircraft

12. covered with stars
13. describing a star or an outstanding performance
14. a group of stars forming a pattern in the sky
15. romantic or idealistic
16. transparent dome for navigators to see the stars

B Compound Words

Solve each equation to come up with a spelling word that is a compound word.

17. star + (someone who stares) =
18. star + (brightness) =
19. star + (sea creature) =
20. star + (tiny particles) =

Spell Chat
Challenge the person next to you to name three other words that contain the word *star* or the root *ast* or *stell*.

Be a Spelling Sleuth

Look for "star" words with the base word *star* or the roots *ast* and *stell* in science books and entertainment magazines.

Spelling Words

stardust	aster
stargazer	asterisk
starlight	asteroid
starboard	disaster
starry-eyed	disastrous
starless	astrodome
star-spangled	astronaut
starfish	astronomy
stellar	astronomer
constellation	astronomical

Review	Challenge
rhythm	astrophysics
visibility	star-studded
lunar	

My Words

_____

_____

_____

Spelling Words

stardust	aster
stargazer	asterisk
starlight	asteroid
starboard	disaster
starry-eyed	disastrous
starless	astrodome
star-spangled	astronaut
starfish	astronomy
stellar LOOKOUT WORD	astronomer
constellation	astronomical

Review	Challenge
rhythm	astrophysics
visibility	star-studded
lunar	

My Words

_____

_____

_____

Quick Write

Use your imagination and "wish upon a star." Describe your wish for the future, using as many "star" words as you can.

A Write a Plan

You may wish to do this activity on a computer.

Think of a dream you have for the future. It might be winning the school science prize, running a marathon, or becoming an astronaut. Outline a plan for how you can make that dream come true. Remember to use proper punctuation at the end of declarative, interrogative, imperative, and exclamatory sentences. Also brainstorm a list of "star" words you might use. Then write your paragraph.

B Proofread

Read the opening of John's plan. He made five spelling errors, two punctuation errors, and one capitalization error. Correct them.

Tip

Remember to use a period to end declarative and imperative sentences, a question mark to end interrogative sentences, and an exclamation mark to end exclamatory sentences.

> Why do people say I'm starry eyed. My dream is to be an astranaut. Here's how I plan to reach my goal First, I will read every book I can find on astranomy. Then, I will continue my study of the constelation orion and observe the moon to chart lunir movement. I'll learn so much on the subject that I'll get into space camp for sure!

PROOFREADING MARKS

∧	Add
⩔	Add a comma
⸌⸍	Add quotation marks
⊙	Add a period
ℓ	Take out
⟳	Move
≡	Capital letter
/	Small letter
¶	Indent

Now proofread your own plan. Check your spelling, punctuation, grammar, and capitalization.

A Use a Dictionary: Syllabication

Each dictionary entry shows you how the word is broken into syllables. Look at the entry for the word *asterisk*. It has three syllables. Every syllable has at least one vowel. Knowing how a word is syllabicated can help you pronounce it.

as•ter•isk /as tə risk/ *noun* The symbol (*) used in printing and writing to tell readers to look elsewhere on the page for more information.

Now write the spelling words *constellation*, *astronaut*, and *astronomical* with their correct syllabication. Then share your words with a partner. Afterward check your work with a dictionary.

_____

_____

B Test Yourself

Each incomplete word below needs *star*, *ast*, or *stell* to make a spelling word. Write each spelling word.

1. ____ dust
2. ____ light
3. ___ erisk
4. ___ eroid
5. ___ er
6. dis ___ er
7. ___ rodome
8. ____ fish
9. ___ ronomy
10. ___ ronomical
11. ____ less
12. ____ gazer
13. _____ ar

14. ____ board
15. con _____ ation
16. dis ___ rous
17. ___ ronaut
18. ____ ry-eyed
19. ___ ronomer
20. ____ -spangled

For Tomorrow...
Get ready to share the **"star"** words you discovered. Don't forget to study for your test!

Get Word Wise

The word *astronaut* contains two Greek roots— *ast*, which means "star," and *naut*, which means "sailor." So an astronaut is someone who "sails" among the stars.

Word Study Strategy

See the word

Say it slowly

Link sounds and letters

Write

Check

END

Spelling Words

baseball
basketball
cheerleader
hallway
homeroom
myself
quarterback
teammate
teenager
air conditioner
a lot *LOOKOUT WORD*
home run
ice cream
locker room
drive-in
light-year
ninety-five
old-fashioned
runner-up
self-defense

Review	Challenge
stellar	upside down
counsel	videocassette
photograph	

My Words

_____

_____

More Compound Words

A See and Say

The Spelling Concept

baseball   home run   runner-up

Compound words are made up of two words that usually stand alone. Compound words can take the form of one word, two words, or two words joined by a hyphen.

> If you have **a lot** of things, you have more than one.

MEMORY JOGGER

B Link Sounds and Letters

Say each spelling word. Listen for the two words that make up each compound word. Then look at each to see whether it takes the form of one word, two words, or two hyphenated words. Write the words in the correct column on a chart like the one below.

Word Sort

One-Word Compounds	Two-Word Compounds	Hyphenated Compounds

C Write and Check

Complete each part of this puzzle with a spelling word.

1. A sport that's played on a wooden court _ _ _ _ _ _ _ _ _ _

2. Subtract the first small word in the above spelling word; add a word that describes what a player touches as he runs around the diamond. _ _ _ _ _ _ _ _

3. Write what every batter hopes for. _ _ _ _ _ _ _

Now use the spelling words to write a word puzzle of your own.

_____

_____

A Build Vocabulary: Related Words

Fill in the blanks with spelling words that fit each group.

- volleyball, football, __1.__ __2.__
- roadway, passageway, __3.__
- twenty-two, forty-one, eighty-seven, __4.__
- bandleader, team leader, __5.__
- self-help, self-esteem, __6.__
- himself, herself, __7.__
- living room, sunroom, __8.__ __9.__
- old-timer, old hat, __10.__
- air bag, air pocket, __11.__

B Word Practice: Compound Words

Solve each equation to come up with a spelling word.

12. coin + opposite of *front* =

13. frozen water + heavy form of milk =

14. marathoner + opposite of *down* =

15. opposite of *dark* + 365 days =

16. go by car + opposite of *out* =

C Write

Write two sentences about a sports event, using the words *home run*, *teammate*, *teenager*, and *a lot*.

___

___

___

Spell Chat

Turn to the person next to you and brainstorm **compound words** about computers and technology. Can either of you come up with a computer term that describes what a mouse uses to take notes?

Be a Spelling Sleuth

Look for more compound words when you read the sports page of a newspaper or a sports magazine. Make lists of sports-related compound words, and note which sport has the most.

Spelling Words

baseball	a lot
basketball	home run
cheerleader	ice cream
hallway	locker room
homeroom	drive-in
myself	light-year
quarterback	ninety-five
teammate	old-fashioned
teenager	runner-up
air conditioner	self-defense

Review	Challenge
stellar	upside down
counsel	videocassette
photograph	

My Words

___
___
___

Spelling Words

baseball	a lot
basketball	home run
cheerleader	ice cream
hallway	locker room
homeroom	drive-in
myself	light-year
quarterback	ninety-five
teammate	old-fashioned
teenager	runner-up
air conditioner	self-defense

Review	Challenge
stellar	upside down
counsel	videocassette
photograph	

My Words

_____

_____

_____

Quick Write

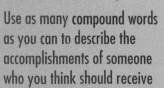

Use as many compound words as you can to describe the accomplishments of someone who you think should receive an award.

A Write an Informative Paragraph

You may wish to do this activity on a computer.

You're a philanthropist—a person who helps others by giving time or money to charities and good causes. Create an award you plan to give someone who has achieved something special. Write an informative paragraph telling what the award would be and who would qualify to receive it. Remember that adjectives will make your writing more interesting. Make a list of compound words that you might use. Then write your paragraph.

B Proofread

Read Kimiko's paragraph describing the requirements for her award. Correct four spelling errors, one usage error, and three capitalization errors.

Tip
When you compare two things, add -er to an adjective; when you compare more than two things, add -est.

The nova Award will be given each year to the most steller young scientist in Webster Middle school. In order to qualify, the teanager must develop an original experiment and show alot of evidence of working hardest than any other student under consideration. Students interested in applying for the award must register immediately. The review committee cannot accept applications after october 10. A runnerup will also be honored.

PROOFREADING MARKS

∧ Add
⋏ Add a comma
⌄ Add quotation marks
⊙ Add a period
ℓ Take out
○↰ Move
≡ Capital letter
/ Small letter
¶ Indent

Now proofread your informative paragraph. Check your spelling, punctuation, capitalization, and grammar.

A Use the Dictionary: Accent Marks

A syllable is a word part that has one vowel sound. If a word has more than one syllable, then one of the syllables is said more strongly, or with more stress. Your Spelling Dictionary uses bold and italic type to show stress. In some words, more than one syllable is stressed. In that case, the syllable with greater stress is shown in bold type and the syllable with lesser stress is shown in italic type, as in the entry for *quarterback* below.

quar•ter•back (kwôr *tər* **bak**) **noun** In football, the player who leads the offense by passing the ball or handing it off to a runner.

Write five spelling words, and then underline the accented syllable in each word. If there are two accented syllables, draw two lines under the syllable with the greater stress. Use your Spelling Dictionary if you wish. Then check your work with a partner.

_____

_____

B Test Yourself

Add the missing part of each compound word. Then write each complete word.

1. base____
2. basket____
3. cheer____
4. hall____
5. ____ room
6. my____
7. quarter____
8. team____
9. teen____
10. air____
11. a____
12. home____
13. ice____
14. locker____
15. drive-____
16. light-____
17. ninety-____
18. old-____
19. runner-____
20. self-____

For Tomorrow...
Get ready to share the compound words you found. Remember to study for your test!

Get Word Wise

The word *basketball* gets its name from the peach baskets that were used in the first version of the game. James Naismith invented basketball in 1891 by attaching two peach baskets to a gymnasium railing, and a new sport was born.

Word Study Strategy

See the word
Say it slowly
Link sounds and letters
Write
Check
END

Learn and Spell

Words With under and sub-

Ⓐ See and Say

The Spelling Concept

under + ground = underground
sub- + marine = submarine

Under and *sub-* both mean "beneath" or "below." *Sub-* can also mean "close to" as in *suburban*—close to the city. Some *under* and *sub-* words have similar meanings; for example, the words *underground* and *subterranean* mean basically the same thing.

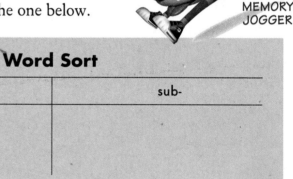

A rabbit's burrow is a subterranean hole.

MEMORY JOGGER

Ⓑ Link Sounds and Letters

Say each spelling word. Listen for *under* or *sub-*. Then write the words in the correct column on a chart like the one below.

Word Sort

under	sub-

Ⓒ Write and Check

Uncover the answers to these questions.

Which spelling word can you substitute for *subterranean*?

_ _ _ _ _ _ _ _ _ _

Which spelling word can you submerge in the sea?

_ _ _ _ _ _ _ _

Now write a question of your own to uncover a spelling word.

_____

_____

_____

Vocabulary Practice

A Build Vocabulary: Synonyms and Antonyms

Synonyms are words that have the same or almost the same meanings. Antonyms are opposites. Write the spelling words that are synonyms or antonyms for the words below.

Synonyms

1. know
2. try
3. underscore
4. topic

Antonyms

5. overpass
6. add
7. aboveground
8. surface

B Word Study: Adverbs and Adjectives

Adverbs can tell where something happens. Adjectives can describe what something is like. Complete each sentence with a spelling word that best tells where something occurs or describes what kind of person or thing it is.

9. The passengers were packed into the (what kind) car like sardines.
10. The (what kind) teacher taught our class for three days.
11. Tania dove (where) and saw a fish.
12. As a (what kind) captain, he spent a lot of time under the sea.
13. The (what kind) policewoman prevented a crime.
14. The puppies were in the way and (where).
15. Mario likes to explore a nearby (what kind) cave.
16. I looked all around the bed and even (where).

C Write

Use the following four spelling words to write sentences about a place you could visit: *subdivision, suburb, suburban, subtropics.*

Be a Spelling Sleuth

Look for under and sub- words in books and magazines about undersea life, or in local newspaper articles about your community. Jot down the words you find.

Spell Chat

Challenge the person next to you to think of other words that begin with **sub-** or **under**. Ask your partner to use each word in a sentence.

Spelling Words

undercover	subject
underfoot	subterranean
underground	submerge
underline	submarine
underpass	substitute
underneath	subtract
understand	subtropics
undertake	suburb
underwater	suburban
subdivision	subway

Review	Challenge
a lot	subordinate
production	subzero
subscribe	

My Words

_____

_____

_____

Spelling Words

undercover	subject
underfoot	subterranean
underground	submerge
underline	submarine
underpass	substitute
underneath	subtract
understand	subtropics
undertake	suburb
underwater	suburban
subdivision	subway

LOOKOUT WORD

Review	Challenge
a lot	subordinate
production	subzero
subscribe	

My Words

_____

_____

_____

Quick Write

Jot down some ideas for a realistic story about an explorer who gets trapped in a cave. Use as many spelling words as you can.

A Write Realistic Fiction

You may wish to do this activity on a computer.

You and several friends are learning to scuba dive. Write a short scene for a realistic story about one of your diving adventures. Use spelling words and other related words to write your story. Include abbreviations for people's initials or for place names.

B Proofread

Read the opening of Doug's story. He made five spelling errors, two punctuation errors, one possessive error, and one capitalization error. Correct them.

Tip

When you write abbreviations or initials, be sure to use periods to stand for the rest of the word, for example, *Mr.* for *Mister* or *B.J.* for *Bob Jones.*

Dr Gonzalez couldn't wait to take T.J and me to the submerine city near the shore of St. bart's. When our little boat reached the coral reef, we put on a lot of diving gear and got ready to submearge. As we slipped underneith the oceans surface, alot of sharks glided into view. We explored the under water city and the marine life that surrounded us.

PROOFREADING MARKS

∧ Add
⋏ Add a comma
∨ Add quotation marks
⊙ Add a period
ℓ Take out
↶ Move
≡ Capital letter
/ Small letter
¶ Indent

Now proofread your story. Check your spelling, grammar, punctuation, and capitalization.

A Use the Dictionary: Respellings

The respelling of an entry word can help you to pronounce it. In some dictionaries, the stressed syllable is written in very dark print. In other dictionaries, an accent mark highlights the stressed syllable. Here's a dictionary entry for the word *subject*.

sub·ject

1. **/sub jikt/** *noun* The person or thing that is discussed or thought about in a book, newspaper article, conversation, etc. 2. *noun* An area of study.
3. **/səb jekt/** *verb* To cause to experience. *Our neighbors subjected us to loud music all night.* ▷ **subjecting, subjected**

Write three of your spelling words with their respellings. Use your Spelling Dictionary to help you.

_____

_____

_____

B Test Yourself

Complete each spelling word with *under* or *sub-*. Then write the complete word.

1. __ cover
2. __ marine
3. __ take
4. __ line
5. __ ject
6. __ merge
7. __ tract
8. __ urb
9. __ ground
10. __ water
11. __ division
12. __ pass

13. __ terranean
14. __ neath
15. __ foot
16. __ stitute

17. __ stand
18. __ tropics
19. __ way
20. __ urban

For Tomorrow...
Get ready to share the **under** and **sub-** words you discovered. Remember to study for your test!

Get Word Wise

The English words *suburb* and *suburban* come from the Latin word *suburbium*. The ancient Romans used the prefix *sub-*, meaning "close to," and the root *urb*, meaning "city," to form the word *suburbium*. Suburbs and *urban* areas have been around for a long time!

f

Word Study Strategy

See the word

Say it slowly

Link sounds and letters

Write

Check

END

Spelling Words

analyze LOOKOUT WORD
advertise
apologize
despise
compromise
disguise
improvise
televise
alphabetize
categorize
criticize
publicize
sympathize
capsize
summarize
emphasize
organize
recognize
realize
utilize

Review	Challenge
subterranean	dramatize
similarity	characterize
exercise	

My Words

_____

_____

Words That End With /īz/

A See and Say

The Spelling Concept

Sound	Spelling	Word
/īz/	-ise	advertise
/īz/	-ize	recognize

Words that end with /īz/ are usually action words, or verbs. The spellings *-ize* and *-ise* stand for /īz/. The spelling *-yze* can also stand for /īz/, as in the word *analyze*.

B Link Sounds and Letters

I spy a y in analyze!

Say each spelling word. Then look at each word to see whether it ends in *-ize, -ise,* or *-yze*. Organize the words on a chart similar to the one below.

MEMORY JOGGER

Word Sort

/īz/ spelled -ize	/īz/ spelled -ise	/īz/ spelled -yze

C Write and Check

The word *television* came first. Then people invented a verb that means "to transmit by television." What do you think this word is?

_ _ _ _ _ _ _ _

Now write a word puzzle for another spelling word.

_____

_____

_____

_____

A Build Vocabulary: Antonyms

An antonym is a word that has the opposite—or nearly the opposite—meaning of another word. *Day* and *night* are antonyms. Use your spelling words to write the antonym for each word below.

1. reveal
2. compliment
3. adore
4. rehearse

B Word Study: Nouns to Verbs

If you know how to spell a noun, you can often spell the verb that's related to it. Write the verbs from your spelling words that are related to the nouns below.

5. utility
6. advertisement
7. alphabet
8. apology
9. emphasis
10. realization
11. recognition
12. analysis
13. summary
14. sympathy
15. category
16. television

Spell Chat

Challenge a person next to you to spell three words that end with /īz/ that are not on your spelling list. Then take your turn to do the same.

C Write

Write three sentences about a sailing trip, using the words *publicize, organize, capsize,* and *compromise.*

_____

_____

_____

_____

_____

Be a Spelling Sleuth

Look for words that end with /īz/, such as *exercise* and *recognize*, on store advertisements and flyers in the mail.

Spelling Words

analyze LOOKOUT WORD	criticize
advertise	publicize
apologize	sympathize
despise	capsize
compromise	summarize
disguise	emphasize
improvise	organize
televise	recognize
alphabetize	realize
categorize	utilize

Review	Challenge
subterranean	dramatize
similarity	characterize
exercise	

My Words

_____

_____

_____

Spelling Words

analyze *LOOKOUT WORD*	criticize
advertise	publicize
apologize	sympathize
despise	capsize
compromise	summarize
disguise	emphasize
improvise	organize
televise	recognize
alphabetize	realize
categorize	utilize

Review	Challenge
subterranean	dramatize
similarity	characterize
exercise	

My Words

_____

_____

_____

Quick Write

Write a two-lined rhyme. Use words from your spelling list with endings that match in spelling as well as in sound.

A **Write a Description**

You may wish to do this activity on a computer.

Look at something very familiar, for a minute or two, as if you'd never seen it before. It can be something small or large. Then write a description of the thing, using details so that someone will see it as clearly as you do.

B **Proofread**

Read the beginning of Erica's description. She made four spelling errors, one capitalization error, one error in subject-verb agreement, and a comma error in a compound sentence. Correct them.

> **Tip**
>
> A compound sentence is made up of two simple sentences. When you write a compound sentence, use a comma before a conjunction such as and, or, or but.

The dark blue drinking glass sits on a snow-white tablecloth near a window. Light from the window pour into the glass and blue light from the glass falls across the white cloth. This light has a simmilarity to the light filtering into a subteranean cave. I was never before able to recognise beauty in an everyday object like this. Now I realise that a blue glass on a white cloth can be like a work of Art.

Now proofread your description. Did you use a comma in a compound sentence? Did you check for errors in spelling, grammar, punctuation, and capitalization?

PROOFREADING MARKS

∧ Add
⁁ Add a comma
ᵛᵛ Add quotation marks
⊙ Add a period
ℓ Take out
◯↗ Move
≡ Capital letter
/ Small letter
¢ Indent

Ⓐ Use a Dictionary: Part of Speech

Here's a dictionary entry for the word *disguise*. Notice the label that shows the part of speech. *Disguise* can be either a verb or a noun. The example sentence following the definition illustrates how the entry word is used as different parts of speech. At the end of the dictionary entry, other related parts of speech are printed in dark type.

dis•guise (dis gīz)

1. *verb* To hide something. *Steve tried to disguise his boredom.* **2. *noun*** Something worn to hide your identity. ***verb*▷ disguising, disguised**

Look up the spelling word *compromise* in your Spelling Dictionary. What parts of speech can this word be? _____. Write one example sentence for each part of speech for *compromise*.

_____

_____

Ⓑ Test Yourself

Add endings to these word beginnings. Then write each complete word. For the last word write the word that has a different ending from the rest.

1. desp _ _ _
2. advert _ _ _
3. apolog _ _ _
4. alphabet _ _ _
5. categor _ _ _
6. comprom _ _ _
7. public _ _ _
8. disgu _ _ _
9. util _ _ _
10. critic _ _ _
11. improv _ _ _
12. summar _ _ _
13. organ _ _ _
14. recogn _ _ _
15. emphas _ _ _
16. telev _ _ _
17. real _ _ _
18. sympath _ _ _
19. caps _ _ _
20. _ _ _ _ _ _ _

For Tomorrow…
Be ready to share some of the words that end in /īz/ that you discovered. Remember to study for your test!

Get Word Wise

The spelling word *alphabetize* means "to put in alphabetical order." It is the verb form of *alphabet*, a word that comes from Greek. The first two letters of the Greek alphabet are *alpha* and *beta*.

Word Study Strategy

See the word
Say it slowly
Link sounds and letters
Write
Check
END

Spelling Words

enemies'
enemy's
that's
let's
he'd
I'd
she'd
couldn't
wouldn't
o'clock — LOOKOUT WORD
first-rate
half-mast
hand-me-down
second-rate
self-control
single-handed
weather-beaten
web-footed
well-balanced
well-behaved

Review	Challenge
analyze	double-header
commitment	freeze-dried
it's	

My Words

_____
_____
_____

Words With Apostrophes and Hyphens

A See and Say

The Spelling Concept

enemy's   that's   first-rate

Apostrophes are used in the possessive form of a noun. Apostrophes are also used in contractions to take the place of a missing letter or letters. Hyphens are used in some compound nouns and adjectives.

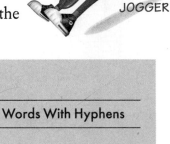

Don't shed the apostrophe in **she'd**.

MEMORY JOGGER

B Link Sounds and Letters

Say each spelling word. Look to see how the apostrophe or hyphen is used in the word. Then sort the spelling words on a chart like the one below.

Word Sort		
Possessive Nouns	Contractions	Words With Hyphens

C Write and Check

Can you figure out the answer to the joke? Write your own joke or riddle, using one or more of the spelling words.

_____
_____
_____

JOKE

What time is it when the clock strikes thirteen o'clock?

Time to get the clock fixed.

A Build Vocabulary: Contractions

Write the spelling word that is a contraction for each word below. What letter or letters in the original words are dropped and replaced by an apostrophe?

1. could + not

2. that + is

3. he + had

4. let + us

5. I + would

6. she + had

7. would + not

8. of + the + clock

Be a Spelling Sleuth

Look for contractions in the dialogue spoken by characters in a short story or novel. Also listen for how people use contractions in their everyday speech.

B Word Study: Adjectives With Hyphens

A hyphen is often used to connect two or more words that are being used together as an adjective. Complete each sentence below with a spelling word that is used as an adjective.

9. She wore _____ clothes from her older sister.

10. The old house by the sea was covered with _____ shingles.

11. The top athlete wanted to attend a college that had a _____ football team.

12. The forest ranger made a _____ effort to control the fire by himself.

13. A mallard duck is one of the most colorful _____ birds.

14. Only young people who were _____ were allowed into the violist's concert.

15. He regretted hiring a painter who did _____ work.

16. The runner always ate _____ meals.

Spell Chat

Challenge a partner to think of four other contractions. Then tell what words they combine.

C Write

Write two sentences about an adventure at sea, using these four spelling words: *enemy's, enemies', half-mast, self-control*.

_____

_____

_____

_____

Spelling Words

enemies'	first-rate
enemy's	half-mast
that's	hand-me-down
let's	second-rate
he'd	self-control
I'd	single-handed
she'd	weather-beaten
couldn't	web-footed
wouldn't	well-balanced
o'clock	well-behaved

Review	Challenge
analyze	double-header
commitment	freeze-dried
it's	

My Words

_____

_____

_____

Spelling Words

enemies'	first-rate
enemy's	half-mast
that's	hand-me-down
let's	second-rate
he'd	self-control
I'd	single-handed
she'd	weather-beaten
couldn't	web-footed
wouldn't	well-balanced
o'clock LOOKOUT WORD	well-behaved

Review	Challenge
analyze	double-header
commitment	freeze-dried
it's	

My Words

_____

_____

_____

Quick Write

Write the opening paragraph of a review of a movie or play you've seen. Include several of the spelling words.

Write and Proofread

A Write a Description

You may wish to do this activity on a computer.

You have just attended a play. Write a short description of your favorite scene or scenes. Include spelling words and other related words in your description. Use a semicolon to separate two related sentences.

B Proofread

Read the beginning of Lee's play description. He made five spelling errors, one punctuation error, and one capitalization error. Help him correct them.

Tip

Be sure to separate two related sentences with a semicolon.

> Was I ever excited when my mother said shed give me tickets to see the play the Farewell Dinner! I knew that its a musical about a man leaving on a trip around the world. My favorite scene was when the man's friends said they wouldnn't let him go and tried to lock him in the house. I liked the dialogue best, the stirring music and sensational costumes also impressed me. The play lasted until eleven oc'lock, but I never got tired. I didn't want to say farewell to the firstrate actors when it was over.

PROOFREADING MARKS

∧	Add
⋏	Add a comma
⸌⸍	Add quotation marks
⊙	Add a period
ℓ	Take out
⌒	Move
≡	Capital letter
/	Small letter
¶	Indent

Now proofread your description. Check your spelling, grammar, punctuation, and capitalization.

A Use the Dictionary: Example Sentence

Here's a dictionary entry for the word *self-control*. It contains an example sentence, which appears after the definition. An example sentence shows the correct use of the word in context.

> **self-con•trol** /self kən trōl/ *noun*
>
> Control of your feelings or behavior. *The boy showed great self-control during the long lecture.* ▷ *adjective* **self-controlled**

Write your own example sentences for two spelling words from this lesson, using each word in context. Underline the spelling words.

_____

_____

_____

_____

B Test Yourself

Write the complete spelling words correctly by adding the missing apostrophe or hyphen to each.

1. enemies
2. enemys
3. thats
4. lets
5. hed
6. Id
7. shed
8. couldnt
9. wouldnt
10. oclock
11. firstrate
12. halfmast
13. handmedown
14. secondrate
15. selfcontrol
16. singlehanded
17. weatherbeaten
18. webfooted
19. wellbalanced
20. wellbehaved

Get Word Wise

The spelling word *enemy's* is the possessive form of the word *enemy*. Enemy comes from the Old French word based on the Latin word *inimicus*. This Latin word was formed from *in* (meaning "not") and *amicus* (meaning "friend").

Word Study Strategy

See the word

Say it slowly

Link sounds and letters

Write

Check

END

For Tomorrow...

Get ready to share the contractions you discovered. Remember to study for the test!

The Universe Series

Fill each blank with a word from the box.

starry-eyed	**baseball**	**astronomical**
ninety-five	**constellation**	**home run**

It is the year two thousand two hundred and __(1)__ . The great American game of __(2)__ is still being played all over the universe! The game has an __(3)__ number of fans in every __(4)__ . Hopeful, __(5)__ youngsters from every planet dream about hitting a __(6)__ far into outer space.

Star-Spangled	**underneath**	**let's**
single-handed	**teammate**	**enemies'**

Now __(7)__ join the fans at the Universe Series held __(8)__ the lights of Milky Way Stadium. The Space Cadets and the Star Walkers have taken the field after singing the __(9)__ Banner. The first eight innings are scoreless. Then the ace batter for the Star Walkers hits the ball out of the stadium with the bases loaded, a great __(10)__ effort. The players mob their __(11)__ as he runs across home plate. The __(12)__ team is glum.

undertake	**realize**	**disaster**
couldn't	**runner-up**	**a lot**

As the Space Cadets come up to bat, they __(13)__ that they have __(14)__ of work ahead of them. They __(15)__ be in a worse position. They __(16)__ a brave effort to score in the last inning, but three straight batters strike out. It's a __(17)__ for the Space Cadets. Once again, the team is the __(18)__ in the Universe Series.

People, Places, and Things

Nouns name a person, place, or thing. Write the Review Words associated with each of the following meanings.

People

teammate   stargazer   astronaut

1. a traveler in space _____

2. a dreamer _____

3. a fellow player _____

Places

homeroom   subdivision   starboard

4. where sailors are found _____

5. a lot for building homes _____

6. where students begin each day _____

Things

baseball   air conditioner   basketball

7. an invention to keep cool _____

8. a game played on a court _____

9. a game played on a diamond _____

Compound Words

Several of the nouns on this page are compound words. How many can you identify? Write the compound words.

10. _____   14. _____

11. _____   15. _____

12. _____   16. _____

13. _____

TRY THIS

Each of these smaller words can be found in at least two spelling words. Can you find them? Write the words.

star _____

_____

run _____

_____

under _____

_____

ball _____

_____

recognize	subtract
o'clock	understand
enemies'	he'd
emphasize	subterranean
disguise	submerge
suburban	myself
astronomer	compromise
apologize	I'd
enemy's	asteroid
underline	disaster
she'd	substitute
well-balanced	

Tip
Remember that an apostrophe takes the place of a missing letter or missing letters in a contraction.

Headlines

Newspapers use headlines that grab your attention. For example, "The Disaster They Couldn't Stop!" Write headlines for the newspaper articles below, using at least two spelling words in each.

1. A space scientist makes a mistake:_____

_____

2. A deep sea diver describes her job:_____

_____

3. A strange rock from outer space is found underground:_____

_____

4. The false identity of a movie star is revealed:_____

_____

5. People leave suburbs for farms:_____

_____

6. Health experts tell what's wrong with diets:_____

_____

7. It's time for Daylight Savings Time:_____

_____

Look back at the words you misspelled on your Unit 3 Posttests. Use them to write two more headlines.

_____

_____

Write All About It!

Write a short newspaper article based on one of your headlines. In your article, answer the questions *who? what? when? where?* and *why?* Proofread the article for spelling, capitalization, and punctuation.

PROOFREADING MARKS

∧	Add
⋏	Add a comma
⌄⌄	Add quotation marks
⊙	Add a period
ℓ	Take out
◯⌒	Move
≡	Capital letter
/	Small letter
¢	Indent

Verbs That End With /īz/

Read what Trevor says. Then write the correct word in each sign.

> analyze · alphabetize · apologize · compromise
> criticize · despise · recognize · realize

1.

Want the best sports equipment?

Don't _____ your standards. Come view our great selection of athletic gear!

2.

This store is **CLOSED** for two weeks for remodeling. We

_____

for any inconvenience.

3.

Save **TIME** and **MONEY.**

We will _____ your income taxes for a reasonable fee.

4.

Do you _____ household chores? Find out about our cleaning service.

5.

Get organized! We can file your papers,

_____

your mailing lists, and organize your office!

6.

Do people

_____

your clothes? **Maybe they're right! Come in and buy a new wardrobe.**

7.

Do you _____ that there are only **10 shopping days** left? Hurry in for a top selection of presents.

8.

Try our make-over special. **You won't**

_____

the new you.

Trevor says...

Words that end in *-ise* and *-ize* can be really tricky to spell. I found that out for myself one day when I went past a delicatessen that my neighbor owns. He had put a sign in his window that read: "We emphasise quality in our food. Try us for the best sandwiches in town!" I recognized right away that he had misspelled *emphasize*. He used an *-ise* ending instead of an *-ize* ending. I didn't want him to be embarrassed by his spelling, so I ran into the deli and politely told him about the mistake in his sign. He thanked me and changed the spelling. Best of all, he gave me a great sandwich as a reward.

Spelling Matters!

Spelling Words

- chiefs *LOOKOUT WORD*
- sheriffs
- ourselves
- themselves
- thieves
- calves
- dominoes
- echoes
- heroes
- potatoes
- volcanoes
- ratios
- solos
- stereos
- quizzes
- series
- species
- mothers-in-law
- brothers-in-law
- media

Review	Challenge
o'clock	data
rhyme	parentheses
bases	

My Words

_____

_____

_____

Uncommon Plurals

A See and Say

The Spelling Concept

calf	calves	potato	potatoes
chief	chiefs	quiz	quizzes
solo	solos	medium	media
		series	series

Some nouns have unusual plurals. Some nouns that end in f change to v before adding es, but others don't. Some nouns that end in o add es to make the plural. Others simply add s. Some nouns double the last letter before adding es. Other nouns, especially those that come from Latin, change from *um* to *a* in the plural. Still other nouns are exactly the same in the singular and plural.

*You can find eyes in pota**toes**, but can you find **toes**?*

MEMORY JOGGER

B Link Sounds and Letters

Say each spelling word. Look and listen for its plural ending. Then write each word on a chart similar to the one below.

Word Sort

Change f to v and Add es	Add s	Add es (May need to Double a Letter)	Same Singular and Plural	Change um to a	Other

C Write and Check

Write a sentence that includes the spelling word that answers the Brain Teaser. Then create your own brain teaser for another spelling word.

_____

_____

_____

BRAIN TEASER

Which spelling word does not have a singular form?

themselves

A Build Vocabulary: Plurals

Complete each sentence. Write the spelling word that is the plural of the noun in parentheses.

1. (domino) Juan and Betty enjoy playing ____.
2. (solo) A few students sang ____ in the concert.
3. (volcano) The Pacific Islands have many active ____.
4. (quiz) We studied for two ____ in English class.
5. (potato) Would you like to eat ____ with your chicken?
6. (hero) On Veterans Day we honor the ____ who defended our country at war.
7. (species) Dogs and wolves belong to different ____.
8. (thief) The ____ broke into the house and stole a stereo.
9. (series) My favorite actor starred in three TV ____.
10. (calf) The cows stayed close to their ____ in the pasture.

B Word Study: Word Meanings

Match the spelling words to the definitions below. Then write the correct spelling words.

11. leaders
12. sound systems with two or more channels of sound
13. different means of communicating information
14. them and no one else
15. law enforcers in a county
16. us and no one else
17. mothers through marriage
18. repeated sounds
19. comparisons of two numbers
20. brothers through marriage

Be a Spelling Sleuth

Look for uncommon plurals in different kinds of stores. Try food shops, toy stores, and music stores for a start. You might find *potatoes, dominoes, solos,* and many more common words that have uncommon plurals.

Spell Chat

Think of two more **uncommon plurals**. Challenge the person next to you to spell the singular and plural forms of your words.

Spelling Words

chiefs	volcanoes
sheriffs	ratios
ourselves	solos
themselves	stereos
thieves	quizzes
calves	series
dominoes	species
echoes	mothers-in-law
heroes	brothers-in-law
potatoes	media

LOOKOUT WORD

Review	Challenge
o'clock	data
rhyme	parentheses
bases	

My Words

_____

_____

_____

Spelling Words

chiefs	volcanoes
sheriffs *(LOOKOUT WORD)*	ratios
ourselves	solos
themselves	stereos
thieves	quizzes
calves	series
dominoes	species
echoes	mothers-in-law
heroes	brothers-in-law
potatoes	media

Review	Challenge
o'clock	data
rhyme	parentheses
bases	

My Words

_____

_____

_____

Quick Write

Write a two-sentence idea for a myth explaining why it rains. Try to use several spelling words in your sentences.

A Write an Idea for a Myth

You may wish to do this activity on a computer.

Imagine that your class is having "The Greatest Myth" contest. Write an idea for a myth. Include a description of the characters.

B Proofread

Frank wrote a retelling of the Greek myth of Echo and Narcissus. He made four spelling errors, one punctuation error, and one usage error. Correct them.

> **Tip**
> Use the word *sit* to denote a person sitting. Use *set* for putting or placing something down.

This Greek myth explains the origins of the words *echo* and *narcissus*. Echo loved the handsome boy named Narcissus, but he rejected her. Through a strange serees of events, Echo could only repeat what anyone said to her. That is why Echo's name was given to the echos we hear. Narcissus fell in love with his own reflection in the water He set down by the water and just kept gazing at his own image. Early one morning, around five oclock', he was transformed into a flower. This flower and many related specees are named for Narcissus.

PROOFREADING MARKS

∧ Add
⅄ Add a comma
⌄⌄ Add quotation marks
⊙ Add a period
ℓ Take out
↶ Move
≡ Capital letter
/ Small letter
¶ Indent

Now proofread your myth. Check for errors in spelling, punctuation, and usage. Did you use *set* and *sit* correctly?

A Use the Dictionary: Word Origins

Word origins tell you the source of a word—what word and language the word comes from, the meaning of the original word, and other interesting information about the word's origin. The origin of a word often comes at the end of a word entry in the dictionary and may be set off by brackets. In this sample entry, find the origin of *volcano*. Then answer the questions.

> **vol·ca·no** /vol kā nō/ *noun*
>
> A mountain with vents through which molten lava, ash, cinders, and gas erupt, sometimes violently. [Italian *volcano*, from Latin *Vulcanus*, meaning Vulcan, Roman god of fire]

What languages does *volcano* come from?

_____   _____

What fictional person is *volcano* named after? _____

B Test Yourself

Fill in the blanks to complete each spelling word. Then write the complete word.

1. her _ _ _
2. thie _ _ _
3. ech _ _ _
4. broth _ _ _ -in-law
5. spec _ _ _
6. potat _ _ _
7. rat _ _ _
8. sol _ _
9. them _ _ _ _ _ _
10. chie _ _
11. moth _ _ _ -in-law
12. volcan _ _ _
13. domin _ _ _
14. med _ _

15. cal _ _ _
16. ster _ _ _
17. quiz _ _ _
18. sheri _ _ _
19. oursel _ _ _
20. ser _ _ _

For Tomorrow...
Bring your own list of words with **uncommon plurals** to share with the class. Remember to study for your test!

Word Study Strategy

See the word

Say it slowly

Link sounds and letters

Write

Check

END

social
socially
sociable
unsociable
soccer *LOOKOUT WORD*
society
associate
association
locate
location
local
locally
dislocate
relocate
popular
popularly
unpopular
popularity
populate
population

Review	Challenge
sheriffs	overpopulated
asterisk	underpopulated
puzzle	

My Words

Words With the Latin Roots
soc, loc, pop

A See and Say

The Spelling Concept

Root	Root's Meaning	Word	Word's Meaning
soc	companion	social	friendly
loc	place	relocate	move to another place
pop	people	popular	liked by people

Many English words are built on roots that came from Latin, such as soc, loc, and pop. Words with the same root are related in spelling and meaning.

I see two c's in soccer.

MEMORY JOGGER

B Link Sounds and Letters

Say each spelling word. Look for the Latin root. Then write each spelling word in the correct column on a chart like the one below.

Word Sort

soc	loc	pop

C Write and Check

Decode the three nonsense words below. To solve the code, write the letter that comes in the alphabet after each coded letter.

1. She won a ONOTKZQHSX contest. _ _ _ _ _ _ _ _ _ _
2. RNBHZAKD people have more fun! _ _ _ _ _ _ _ _
3. We visited a movie KNBZSHNM in Florida! _ _ _ _ _ _ _ _

Now write your own sentence, using the code.

_____

_____

A Build Vocabulary: Latin Roots

Figure out which Latin root, *soc, loc,* or *pop,* completes each word below. Then write each complete word.

1. ____ular
2. re____ate
3. ____iety
4. ____ulate
5. ____al

6. ____ial
7. ____ccr
8. ____ate
9. un____iable
10. ____ation

B Word Study: Prefixes, Suffixes, and Word Parts

Add prefixes, suffixes, or word parts to roots to form spelling words. Use the clues below. Then write the correct spelling words.

11. root + ending *ially* = _____
12. root + ending *ally* = _____
13. prefix *dis* + root + ending *ate* = _____
14. prefix *un* + root + *ular* = _____
15. prefix *as* + root + ending *iate* = _____
16. root + ending *iable* = _____
17. prefix *as* + root + ending *iation* = _____
18. root + ending *ulation* = _____
19. root + ending *ularity* = _____
20. root + ending *ularly* = _____

Spell Chat

Play a root association game with a partner. One partner picks the root **soc, pop,** or **loc.** The other partner says the first word using that root that comes to mind. Try <u>not</u> to use spelling words.

Spelling Words

social	local
socially	locally
sociable	dislocate
unsociable	relocate
soccer *LOOKOUT WORD*	popular
society	popularly
associate	unpopular
association	popularity
locate	populate
location	population

Review	Challenge
sheriffs	overpopulated
asterisk	underpopulated
puzzle	

My Words

_____
_____
_____

You may wish to do this activity on a computer.

Spelling Words

social	local
socially	locally
sociable	dislocate
unsociable	relocate
soccer LOOKOUT WORD	popular
society	popularly
associate	unpopular
association	popularity
locate	populate
location	population

Review	Challenge
sheriffs	overpopulated
asterisk	underpopulated
puzzle	

My Words

_____

_____

_____

Quick Write

Make up a proverb, or saying, that might be found in a folktale. Use some spelling words in your saying.

A Write About a Lesson Learned

Tell about a lesson you learned from your own experience. Now try to think of a folktale that teaches the same lesson. Write a paragraph describing what happened and what you learned. Include some spelling words and a direct quotation.

B Proofread

Here is the lesson Hilda learned from experience. She made three spelling errors, one capitalization error, and three punctuation errors. Correct them.

Tip
Remember, quotation marks are used to set off a speaker's words from the rest of the sentence.

> My friend sam and I created a garden in the lacation of an ugly vacant lot. First, we had to puzzel out which plants to buy at a lockal greenhouse. Then, we started to plant. I took time to find a sunny place for the plants. Sam planted quickly but his plants didn't do as well. He had to relocate them. "This is like the tale of the tortoise and the hare, I said. Slow and steady gets the job done!"

PROOFREADING MARKS

∧	Add
⸶	Add a comma
ᵛⱽ	Add quotation marks
⊙	Add a period
ℓ	Take out
◯↗	Move
≡	Capital letter
/	Small letter
¶	Indent

Now proofread your paragraph. Check spelling, capitalization, grammar, and punctuation. Be sure to set off any speaker's words in quotation marks.

A Use the Dictionary: Standard and Slang Words

Standard English follows a set of rules. You learn standard English at school, and you're expected to use it when writing and speaking in formal, school, or business settings. Slang, however, involves colorful words that you might use casually with family and friends. Both standard English and slang are acceptable when used in the right setting. Read these entries for a standard word and a slang word.

> **pop·u·lar** /pop yə lər/ *adjective* Liked or enjoyed by many people.
> **cool** /kōol/ *adjective* Socially skillful.

The words *rap* and *heavy* have both standard and slang meanings. Choose one of these words. Write a sentence demonstrating both its standard and slang meanings.

B Test Yourself

Write the spelling words that are defined by these words or phrases.

1. a party
2. site
3. to disturb
4. well-liked
5. a sport
6. partner
7. commonly
8. to inhabit
9. club
10. disliked
11. friendly
12. to move
13. in a local area
14. to find
15. community
16. in the area
17. in a social manner
18. not friendly
19. being well-liked
20. all of the people

For Tomorrow...
Share with the class your words with the roots *soc*, **pop**, and **loc**. Remember to study for the test!

Get Word Wise

Back by *popular* demand! Just what does it mean to be popular? The word *popular* comes from a Latin word meaning "the people." Soccer is a popular sport all over the world.

Word Study Strategy

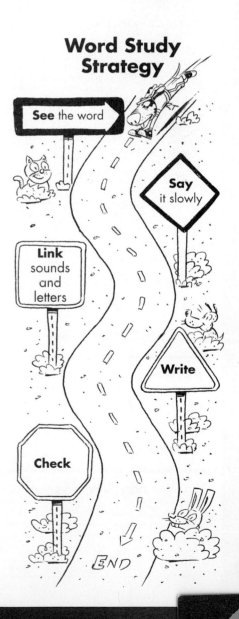

See the word

Say it slowly

Link sounds and letters

Write

Check

END

Latin Roots: *soc, loc, pop*

Spelling Words

supermarket
superior
superhuman
superintendent
supervise
supersonic
superlative *LOOKOUT WORD*
superpower
overcome
overboard
overlook
overhear
overcast
overwhelmed
overdue
overjoyed
overlap
overturn
overtake
overslept

Review	Challenge
soccer	superficial
ninety-five	superimpose
circumstance	

My Words

_____

_____

_____

Words With super and over

Ⓐ See and Say

The Spelling Concept

Super/Over	Word Part/Word Ending	New Word
super	power (base word)	= superpower
super	ior (word part)	= superior
over	look (base word)	= overlook

Super and *over* are base words. They mean "more than, greater than, above and beyond." They can be combined with other base words (*overlook*) or word parts (*superior*) to make new words. The new words include the meaning of *super* or *over* in their definitions.

Ⓑ Link Sounds and Letters

Say each spelling word. Listen for *super* or *over*. Look to see if the word contains a base word or a word part. Then sort the words on a chart like this one.

My trip wasn't just SUPER; it was SUPERlative!

MEMORY JOGGER

Word Sort

super		over	
super + another base word	super + word part	over + another base word	over + base word with past-tense ending

Ⓒ Write and Check

Complete the sentences below. In the spaces, write the spelling word that is suggested by the underlined clue words. Then write your own sentence that includes a clue to a spelling word.

1. Have you ever _____ after having a <u>sleep over</u>?

2. <u>Look over</u> your answers to the math problems, because you could _____ a mistake.

_____

A Build Vocabulary: Words With *super* and *over*

Which base word, *super* or *over*, will help you form the spelling words in this lesson? Use the clues to help you create each spelling word. Write the entire word.

1. faster than the speed of sound   _____ sonic
2. falling over the side of a ship   _____ board
3. beyond people's strength   _____ human
4. place to buy more than just groceries   _____ market
5. beyond joyful   _____ joyed
6. strongly affected by   _____ whelmed
7. greater than the best   _____ lative
8. cloudy and dark   _____ cast
9. beyond the deadline   _____ due
10. nation more powerful than others   _____ power
11. the highest quality   _____ ior
12. slept too long   _____ slept
13. person who oversees things   _____ intendent

B Word Study: Present-Tense Verbs

Here are some verbs in the past tense. Change them to verbs in the present tense.

14. supervised
15. overlapped
16. overcame
17. overturned
18. overlooked
19. overtook
20. overheard

Be a Spelling Sleuth

Look for words that contain super or over in science fiction comics or on movie posters. Keep a list of the words you find.

Spelling Words

supermarket	overlook
superior	overhear
superhuman	overcast
superintendent	overwhelmed
supervise	overdue
supersonic	overjoyed
superlative *LOOKOUT WORD*	overlap
superpower	overturn
overcome	overtake
overboard	overslept

Review	Challenge
soccer	superficial
ninety-five	superimpose
circumstance	

My Words

_____

_____

_____

Spell Chat

With a partner, suggest some **super** or **over** words you've heard or read but whose meanings you don't know, such as *supercilious*. Then look up the meanings of the words in a dictionary. (*supercilious*—haughty or snobbish)

Spelling Words

supermarket	overlook
superior	overhear
superhuman	overcast
superintendent	overwhelmed
supervise	overdue
supersonic	overjoyed
superlative	overlap
superpower	overturn
overcome	overtake
overboard	overslept

Review	Challenge
soccer	superficial
ninety-five	superimpose
circumstance	

My Words

_____

_____

_____

Quick Write

Use as many spelling words as you can to write a list of qualities you most admire in a superhero.

A Write About a Fantasy

You may wish to do this activity on a computer.

Who's your favorite book or movie superhero? What accomplishment of this person do you particularly remember? Write a paragraph telling about that fantastic accomplishment.

B Proofread

Proofread the first draft of Kristina's paragraph. There are four spelling errors, one punctuation error, and two errors in pronoun-antecedent agreement. Correct them.

Tip
Pronouns must agree with their antecedents in gender and number.

> Superman is my favorite movie superhero. No matter what the circumstence, it always manages to perform suprahuman feats. In one spectacular movie scene, she actually had to ovortake the passage of time to save Lois Lane from destruction. The whole audience was overjoyd. Superman succeeded once again

Now proofread your own paragraph. Check spelling, grammar, capitalization, and punctuation. Be sure your pronouns and antecedents agree.

PROOFREADING MARKS

∧ Add
⅄ Add a comma
ⱽⱽ Add quotation marks
⊙ Add a period
ℓ Take out
◯↗ Move
≡ Capital letter
╱ Small letter
¶ Indent

A Use the Dictionary: Guide Words

Guide words appear at the top of each dictionary page. They tell you the first and last entry words, in alphabetical order, that appear on the page. Read the guide words on the sample dictionary page below. Then write the words from the following list that could appear on this page in alphabetical order.

something ▶ supermarket

sundown, sun, sudden, sultry, sundial, superhuman, supermodern, sun-baked, summon, sunfish, superagent, superintendent, superachiever, super mom, superintelligent, supersafe, supersharp

_____

_____

_____

_____

B Test Yourself

Write the spelling words that could be on the same page as each set of guide words below. Then alphabetize the words for each page, and write them in that order.

superman/superwide
1. _____
2. _____
3. _____
4. _____

superhero/superlunary
13. _____
14. _____
15. _____
16. _____

overserious/overzealous
17. _____
18. _____
19. _____
20. _____

overhasty/overlord
5. _____
6. _____
7. _____
8. _____

overbake/overeat
9. _____
10. _____
11. _____
12. _____

For Tomorrow...
Share the **over** and **super** words you found in science fiction comics or on movie posters. Remember to study for your test!

Get Word Wise

The word *overwhelm* originated in Middle English hundreds of years ago. *Whelmen* meant "to turn," and when the combining form over was added, it became *overwhelmen*, "to cover over completely." Today overwhelm may mean "to overcome or overpower" or "to turn over, upset."

Word Study Strategy

See the word

Say it slowly

Link sounds and letters

Write

Check

END

Spelling Words

digest
digestion
exclaim
exclamation
explain
explanation
erode
erosion
extend
extension
compose
composition
divide
division
multiply
multiplication LOOKOUT WORD
duplicate
duplication
observe
observation

Review	Challenge
superlative	simplify
underneath	simplification
situation	

My Words

_____

_____

More Suffixes -ation and -ion

A See and Say

The Spelling Concept

Verb	Spelling Changes	Suffix	Noun
digest		ion	digestion
multiply	-y + ic	ation	multiplication
divide	-de + s	ion	division

The suffixes -*ation* and -*ion* are added to many verbs to form nouns. In some words, a letter or letters are added, dropped, or changed before adding the suffix.

Explain loses its i when it becomes explanation.

MEMORY JOGGER

B Link Sounds and Letters

Say each spelling word. Listen for the ending -*ation* or -*ion* in each noun formed from the verb. Then sort the spelling words on a chart like the one below. Put an asterisk (*) next to the word if the base word does not change when you add the suffix.

Word Sort

Verbs	Nouns With Suffix -*ation*	Nouns With Suffix -*ion*

C Write and Check

You'll need sharp eyes for this one! Write the spelling words in which each of the following words can be found. For example, the word *ply* can be found in the spelling word *multiply*.

tension   vision   claim

1. _____   2. _____   3. _____

Now use the three spelling words to write sentences.

A Build Vocabulary: **Word Families**

Word families are groups of related words that share the same root or base word. Read each word below. Then write a spelling word that is in its word family. Here's the trick—make sure your spelling word is a verb!

1. multiplying
2. extended
3. exclaiming
4. composer
5. duplicating
6. eroding
7. explained
8. undigested
9. dividing
10. observant

B Word Study: **Word Clues**

Read the word clues below. Write the spelling word that has a meaning similar to each clue.

11. a remark
12. an addition
13. absorption
14. separation
15. wearing away
16. increase
17. reproduction
18. a shout
19. makeup of something
20. interpretation

C Write

Have you ever had to explain something in writing? Then you've written an explanation. Write a sentence below that tells about your explanation and uses the word *explanation*.

_____

_____

_____

Be a Spelling Sleuth

Look for words with the suffixes -ation and -ion in your math and science textbooks, as well as in science magazines.

Spell Chat

Turn to the person next to you and challenge him or her to think of other words that relate to two of the spelling words.

Spelling Words

digest	compose
digestion	composition
exclaim	divide
exclamation	division
explain	multiply
explanation	multiplication
erode	duplicate
erosion	duplication
extend	observe
extension	observation

Review	Challenge
superlative	simplify
underneath	simplification
situation	

My Words

_____

_____

_____

Spelling Words

digest	compose
digestion	composition
exclaim	divide
exclamation	division
explain	multiply
explanation	multiplication (LOOKOUT WORD)
erode	duplicate
erosion	duplication
extend	observe
extension	observation

Review	Challenge
superlative	simplify
underneath	simplification
situation	

My Words

____

____

____

Quick Write

Use as many words with -ation and -ion as you can to write a funny description of a science project.

Write and Proofread

You may wish to do this activity on a computer.

A Write Humorous Fiction

Your class is preparing for a science fair when you and a friend discover that you're working on the same project! Write a fictional description about how you solve the problem, and give the solution a humorous twist. Use several spelling words.

B Proofread

Proofread Tandra's account of the science fair problem. She made four spelling errors, one capitalization error, and three punctuation errors. Correct them.

Tip
Use quotation marks to set off a speaker's words.

kyra and I had been working on our science fair projects for two weeks when I made the observasion that we had a duplacasion of projects – we had both chosen to study the same kind of rock.

What a situasion! I exclaimed. "How will we explian it to our teacher?"

We didn't want to start over, so we met and went rock collecting together. Unfortunately I slipped and fell into a muddy stream. I decided to do a nice indoor study on the effect of music on plant growth!

PROOFREADING MARKS

- ∧ Add
- ∧ Add a comma
- Add quotation marks
- ⊙ Add a period
- Take out
- Move
- ≡ Capital letter
- / Small letter
- ¶ Indent

Now proofread your own writing. Check for spelling, grammar, capitalization, and punctuation.

Ⓐ Use the Dictionary: Multiple Meanings

Many words have more than one meaning. In a dictionary, each meaning of a word is numbered and defined separately. Study this dictionary entry for *extend*.

> **ex•tend** /ik stend/ *verb*
>
> **1.** To make something longer or bigger. *The frog extended its tongue, catching the beetle.* **2.** To stretch out; reach. *Our yard extends to the lake.* **3.** To offer something, as in *to extend help to flood victims.*
> ▷ **extending, extended** ▷ *noun* **extension**

Write a sentence for each dictionary meaning of the word *extend*.

_____

_____

Ⓑ Test Yourself

Write the spelling word that fits each definition.

1. to split into parts
2. the act of making an exact copy
3. the wearing away of something
4. to give a reason for something
5. the process of breaking down food in the stomach
6. the act of dividing one number by another
7. to grow in number or amount
8. something you notice by watching
9. to wear away by water or wind
10. to make an exact copy
11. to say something suddenly and with force
12. an addition to something
13. to write music or a poem
14. a reason given
15. the makeup or design of something
16. to watch something or someone carefully
17. to stretch or reach out
18. to break down food in the stomach
19. the process of making a number grow
20. an expression of surprise or excitement

For Tomorrow...
Bring your list of science and math words with **-ation** and **-ion** to class. Remember to study for your test!

Get Word Wise

Multiply comes from the Latin word *multiplicare*. The Romans believed that increasing a number by itself several times was like folding a piece of cloth—the more folds, the greater the number. *Multiplicare* comes from *plicare*, "to fold," and *multus*, which means "many."

Word Study Strategy

See the word

Say it slowly

Link sounds and letters

Write

Check

END

Spelling Words

- exterior
- interior
- express
- impress
- expression
- impression
- external
- internal
- exhale
- inhale
- exportation
- importation
- extinct
- instinct
- exhibit *LOOKOUT WORD*
- inhibit
- exclude
- include
- exclusion
- inclusion

Review	Challenge
multiplication	emigration
summarize	immigration
excite	

My Words

_____

_____

_____

Learn and Spell

Words With Prefixes ex- and in-

A See and Say

The Spelling Concept

Prefix	Meaning	Word	Meaning
ex-	out	exclude	to keep out
in-	in, on, or inward	interior	inner part of something
im-	in, on, or inward	impression	a feeling or idea

The prefixes *ex-* and *in-* or *im-* have opposite meanings. *Ex-* means "out or outward," and *in-* or *im-* means "in, on, or inward." Adding these prefixes to a root changes the meaning of the root. Note that *in-* becomes *im-* before the letter *p*.

> Air **exits** when you **exhale**, and goes **in** when you **inhale**.

B Link Sounds and Letters

Say each spelling word. Look at the beginning of each word to see how the prefix is spelled. On a chart like the one below, sort the spelling words according to their prefixes.

MEMORY JOGGER

Word Sort

ex-	in-	im-

C Write and Check

To answer the riddle, find two spelling words that begin with *ex-*. Now write a riddle of your own, using two other spelling words.

_____

_____

RIDDLE

What is another way to describe a dinosaur display?

An extinct exhibit

A Build Vocabulary: Predicate Adjectives

A predicate adjective follows a linking verb and describes the subject of the sentence. In the sentences that follow, each missing predicate adjective is a spelling word. Write the missing words.

1. The building's clock is _____ ; it is located on the outside wall.

2. The car's damage is _____ ; the inside is fine.

3. Your heart and lungs are _____ .

4. That species of bird is _____ .

B Word Study: Prefixes

Think of the correct prefix to complete the spelling word in each sentence. Write the spelling word.

5. They hired an ____terior decorator.

6. Her ____stinct is always correct.

7. She used a funny ____pression in her speech.

8. Did you enjoy the art ____hibit?

9. Our government regulates the ____portation of goods from other countries.

10. She made a good first ____pression on the new teacher.

11. Try to ____press yourself clearly in your writing.

12. Japan is known for its ____portation of cars.

13. Take a deep breath and then ____hale.

14. The presence of the audience might ____hibit her.

15. He did his best to ____press the baseball coach.

16. Be careful not to ____hale toxic fumes.

17. She did not ____clude Maria from the games.

18. The ____clusion of Sandy in our club is a good idea.

19. I want to ____clude everyone in my class.

20. I think the ____clusion of Benjy was unfair.

Spell Chat

Challenge a partner to spell all the **ex-** words. Then you spell all the **in-** or **im-** words. Did you both get them all right?

Be a Spelling Sleuth

Experiment and *immune* are examples of words with the prefixes ex- and im- that can be found in science or health books. Look in your science textbook and in health books and magazines for words with the prefixes ex- and in- or im-. Keep a list of the words you find.

Spelling Words

exterior	exportation
interior	importation
express	extinct
impress	instinct
expression	exhibit
impression	inhibit
external	exclude
internal	include
exhale	exclusion
inhale	inclusion

Review	Challenge
multiplication	emigration
summarize	immigration
excite	

My Words

_____

_____

_____

Spelling Words

exterior	exportation
interior	importation
express	extinct
impress	instinct
expression	exhibit
impression	inhibit
external	exclude
internal	include
exhale	exclusion
inhale	inclusion

LOOKOUT WORD

Review	Challenge
multiplication	emigration
summarize	immigration
excite	

My Words

_____

_____

_____

Quick Write

To persuade a friend to visit your favorite place, write down several important features of that place, or several fun things to do there. Use words with the prefixes ex- and in- or im-.

A Write a Comparison

You may wish to do this activity on a computer.

Write two paragraphs in which you compare or contrast your two favorite places. You could compare two countries, or just two rooms! Make sure that you indent each paragraph.

B Proofread

Proofread Tranh's paragraphs about New York and New Orleans. Find four spelling errors, one error in capitalization, one in punctuation, and one other error. Correct the errors.

Tip
Remember, the first word of a paragraph is indented. It starts several spaces in from the left margin.

> The two cities that exite me most are New York and New Orleans. My strongest impresion of New York is its quick pace, which makes me feel really alive. I'll never forget my visit to the Empire State Building and my boat tour around Manhattan
>
> New Orleans has city life like New York, but it also has old, graceful homes. Mostly, I like its relaxed mood. I can visit the intearior of jackson Square and study the exibits of the sidewalk artists. Nowhere else on Earth do the people make better seafood gumbo!

Now proofread your writing. Check spelling, grammar, capitalization, and punctuation. Have you indented your paragraphs?

PROOFREADING MARKS

∧   Add

⋏   Add a comma

ᐯᐯ   Add quotation marks

⊙   Add a period

ℓ   Take out

↻   Move

≡   Capital letter

╱   Small letter

¢   Indent

Ⓐ Use the Dictionary: Pronunciation

After every entry word in the dictionary you will find the pronunciation. Look at the dictionary entry for the word *exportation*.

ex·por·ta·tion /ek spôr tā shən/ *noun*
The act of sending products to another country to be sold there.

Write the pronunciation for each of these spelling words. Use the Spelling Dictionary to help you.

1. exhale _____

2. impress _____

3. interior _____

Ⓑ Test Yourself

Write the spelling word to match each definition.

1. the act of making part of

2. to tell in words

3. the act of sending goods to other countries

4. your feelings or ideas about something

5. to affect the feelings of someone

6. outside part

7. no longer in existence

8. to breathe in

9. outside

10. to hold back

11. to breathe out

12. to display

13. a natural skill or ability

14. the act of bringing goods to a place

15. the act of keeping out

16. a saying

17. to keep out

18. inside

19. to make someone a part of

20. inside part

> **For Tomorrow...**
> Write on a slip of paper three **ex-** and **in-** or **im-** words that you found in health or science books. Remember to study for the test!

Get Word Wise

The words *exportation* and *importation* are opposites. Both come from the Latin root *portare*, which means "to carry." *Exportation* is the act of carrying something out of a place, and *importation* is the act of bringing something into a place.

Word Study Strategy

See the word

Say it slowly

Link sounds and letters

Write

Check

END

MAN OVERBOARD

Complete each paragraph with words from the box.

associate	exclamation	overboard	
overcast	overslept	series	supervise

Captain's Log, 6 October 1789

I was alone on deck. The sky was __(1)__ and of a color so similar to that of the sea, it was impossible to tell where one ended and the other began. My first mate had __(2)__, so it fell to me to __(3)__ the crew until my __(4)__ saw fit to take up his duties. The morning quiet was broken by a __(5)__ of alarming shouts. Then came an __(6)__ of surprise and fear, followed by a splash and the cry, "Man __(7)__!"

sociable	exhibit	expression
overwhelmed	population	society

I rushed to the scene and found the entire __(8)__ of the ship (except for the sleeping first mate) gathered at the rail staring down at the unfortunate man in the water. Every man's face bore an __(9)__ of alarm. The crew seemed __(10)__ by the __(11)__ of panic shown by the crewman in distress. The man overboard was Hathaway, a __(12)__ young man who had just joined our shipboard __(13)__.

impression	overcome	overturn
species	ourselves	

I got the clear __(14)__ that the crew needed leadership to save Hathaway. I ran to __(15)__ a lifeboat and pulled a life preserver from under it. The crew rallied to save their fellow member of the human __(16)__. Suddenly, everyone was __(17)__ with joy. Hathaway was pulled from the water, shaken but alive. The crew and I thought of __(18)__ as heroes.

In and Out

In and *out* are opposites. The prefix *in-* means "in," and the prefix *ex-* means "out." However, words with the prefixes *ex-* and *in-* aren't always opposites. Write the *ex-* and *in-* pairs that go with these meanings.

outside/inside

1. _____

_____

2. _____

_____

to show/to hold back

3. _____

_____

to tell/to affect feelings

4. _____

_____

external

inhibit

exterior

internal

interior

impress

express

exhibit

TRY THIS

Write four words that begin with the prefix *ex-*. Then see if you can change the prefix to *in-* or *im-* to create another real word.

_____

_____

_____

_____

Uncommon Plurals

Read the singular words. Then write the singular and plural forms of each word on the lines below.

	Singular	Plural
sheriff	5. _____	_____
hero	6. _____	_____
potato	7. _____	_____
stereo	8. _____	_____
volcano	9. _____	_____
quiz	10. _____	_____
medium	11. _____	_____

Shipwrecked!

Imagine that you are shipwrecked on a deserted island. Every day you send off a message in a bottle. What do you say? Write your messages for four days. Use several different Review Words in every message.

erode	exclaim
locate	exclamation
locally	erosion
relocate	compose
divide	composition
association	external
overboard	inhibit
overwhelmed	popularity

Tip
Remember that some nouns form their plurals in uncommon ways.

DAY 1 _____
_____
_____

DAY 2 _____
_____
_____

DAY 3 _____
_____
_____

DAY 4 _____
_____
_____

Look back at the words you misspelled on your Unit 4 Posttests. Use them to write another message.

Tell How It Happened

Write a brief explanation of how you ended up shipwrecked in the first place. Proofread your work for spelling, grammar, capitalization, and punctuation.

PROOFREADING MARKS
....

∧   Add
⋏   Add a comma
᭼᭼   Add quotation marks
⊙   Add a period
ℓ   Take out
ᵔ⌒   Move
≡   Capital letter
／   Small letter
¢   Indent

Write It Right

Imagine that you found the messages written below. What would you tell the person sending each message to do? Write your advice. Use a different word in each response.

soccer   **superintendent**

1. Help! There's no hot water in our apartment.

_____

2. I found a black-and-white ball, and I don't know what it's for.

_____

division   **multiplication**

3. How can I find out what half of 560 is?

_____

4. I've learned addition, subtraction, and division. What's left to learn?

_____

supermarket   **multiply**   **superlative**

5. I wrote in my book report that *Martha Speaks* was the most funny book I'd read. Why did my teacher circle "most funny"?

_____

6. Where can I find a bandage, a glass of milk, and paper plates?

_____

7. I know how much one bagel costs. When I go to buy lots of bagels, how will I know how much money to bring?

_____

Moira says...

There's a sign in my apartment building that says, "RING BELL FOR SUPPER." It's on the door to the superintendent's office. I recognized right away that *super* was misspelled. I didn't want the superintendent to be embarrassed by his spelling, so I rang his bell and pointed out the mistake. Can you believe it? The super thanked me and invited me in for *supper*!

Spelling Matters!

Spelling Words

earthbound
earthworm
earthshaking
earthmover
earthling
earthly
earthquake
geography
geographical
geology
geologist
geological
geometry
geometric
terrain
territory
territorial
terrier
terrace
terrarium *LOOKOUT WORD*

Review	Challenge
exhibit	terrestrial
enemy's	terra-cotta
global	

My Words

_____
_____
_____

"Earth" Words

A See and Say

The Spelling Concept

earthquake	a violent shaking of the earth
geology	the study of the earth's crust
terrain	ground or land

Many English words have the base word *earth* in them. Other words are built on Greek or Latin roots that mean "earth." In Greek, *geo* means "of the earth," and in Latin, *terra* means "earth." Words with the same root are related in spelling and meaning.

We hiked the rocky terrain in the rain.

B Link Sounds and Letters

Say each spelling word. Listen for the part of the word that means "earth" or "of the earth." Then sort the words, and write them in a chart like the one below.

MEMORY JOGGER

Word Sort

earth	geo	terra

C Write and Check

Complete the rhyme with a spelling word.

When the plates shake and the glasses break, prepare yourself for a mean _ _ _ _ _ _ _ _ _ _ .

Now use another "earth" word on your spelling list to make up a rhyme.

_____

_____

_____

A Build Vocabulary: Word Meanings

Write the spelling word that best completes each sentence.

1. A book on rock formations is a _____ study.

2. If a cat guards the space around it, it is _____.

3. The map comes with a _____ legend that tells us about countries, landforms, and resources.

4. My aunt studies the earth's rocks and soil; she's a _____.

5. That dump truck is an _____ because it transports dirt from one place to another.

6. The branch of mathematics that deals with lines, angles, and shapes is called _____.

7. A dog that hunts animals that live in burrows is a _____.

8. Triangles and circles are examples of _____ shapes.

B Word Study: Roots

The Greek root *geo* means "of the earth." The Latin root *terra* means "earth." Write the spelling words with these roots defined below.

9. ground or land

10. study of the earth's layers of soil and rock

11. large area of land; region

12. study of the earth, including its people, resources, and climate

13. raised, flat platform of land; patio

14. glass container for growing plants

C Write

Write two funny sentences that together include these six earth words: *earthbound, earthworm, earthshaking, earthling, earthly,* and *earthquake.*

_____

_____

_____

Be a Spelling Sleuth

Look for "earth" words in newspapers, magazine articles, or television reports about the environment. Make a list of "earth" words you see and hear.

Spell Chat

Challenge the person next to you to suggest two other words that include the Greek form *geo.*

Spelling Words

earthbound	geologist
earthworm	geological
earthshaking	geometry
earthmover	geometric
earthling	terrain
earthly	territory
earthquake	territorial
geography	terrier
geographical	terrace
geology	terrarium

Review	Challenge
exhibit	terrestrial
enemy's	terra-cotta
global	

My Words

_____

_____

_____

Spelling Words

earthbound	geologist
earthworm	geological
earthshaking	geometry
earthmover	geometric
earthling	terrain
earthly	territory
earthquake	territorial
geography	terrier
geographical	terrace
geology	terrarium **LOOKOUT WORD**

Review	Challenge
exhibit	terrestrial
enemy's	terra-cotta
global	

My Words

_____

_____

_____

Quick Write

What does an earthquake or an erupting volcano look like? Write a sentence describing one of these sights. Include at least one "earth" word.

A. Write a Description

You may wish to do this activity on a computer.

Imagine that you are a geographer studying the landforms in your area. Write a description of one landform—such as a mountain, valley, or plain—that interests you most. Use spelling words in your description and remember to use capital letters when writing initials and titles.

B. Proofread

Read the beginning of Kaysha's description. She made four spelling errors, two capitalization errors, one punctuation error, and one other error. Correct them.

> **Tip**
> Be sure to capitalize initials and important words in titles.

Not far from my house is Mount st. Helens, an active volcano of interest to gealigists everywhere. The terain of the mountain changed after an eruption in 1980. Today, there are fewer, smaller trees growing on the slopes. Every week there is a report about the mountain in the local newspaper, The Mountain gazette, and every year students prepare an exibit about the volcano? Even earthkwakes don't ultimately change the land as much as erupting volcanoes do.

Now proofread your own description. Check your spelling, grammar, capitalization, and punctuation.

PROOFREADING MARKS

∧	Add
⅄	Add a comma
ᵛ ᵛ	Add quotation marks
⊙	Add a period
ℓ	Take out
⌒⌒	Move
≡	Capital letter
/	Small letter
¢	Indent

A Use the Dictionary: Word Endings

Look at the dictionary entry for *geography*. It also lists the words *geographer* and *geographical*. Words formed by adding a suffix may not appear as separate entry words in the dictionary. To find these words, you have to look up the base word to which the suffix has been added.

---

ge·og·ra·phy /jē og rə fē/ *noun* The study of the earth, including its people, resources, climate, and physical features. ▷ *noun* geographer *adjective* geographical

TEXAS
AUSTIN

Read each of the following words. Write the entry word under which you would find the word listed in some dictionaries.

- territorial _____

- earthly _____

- geologist _____

B Test Yourself

Use the code to find out the root or part of each spelling word that makes it an "earth" word. Then write the "earth" spelling word.

▲ = *earth*　　□ = *geo*　　○ = *terr*

1. ▲ bound
2. □ graphy
3. ○ ain
4. ▲ worm
5. □ graphical
6. ○ itory
7. ▲ shaking
8. □ logy
9. ○ itorial
10. ▲ mover
11. ▲ ly
12. □ logist
13. □ logical
14. ○ ier
15. ○ ace
16. ▲ quake
17. ▲ ling
18. ○ arium
19. □ metry
20. □ metric

For Tomorrow...
Get ready to share your observations about where you read or heard **"earth"** words. Remember to study for your test!

Get Word Wise

As you know, the Latin word *terra* means "earth." In Italian, the term *terra-cotta* means "baked earth," and a *terra-cotta* pot is made from a kind of clay that is baked until it turns reddish "earth" brown in color.

Word Study Strategy

See the word

Say it slowly

Link sounds and letters

Write

Check

END

Spelling Words

form
formal
informal
formality
formula LOOKOUT WORD
formless
format
conform
conforming
inform
informally
information
informational
informative
uninformed
reform
reforming
uniform
transform
transformation

Review	Challenge
terrarium	misinform
volcanoes	misinformation
performance	

My Words

_____

_____

Word Family form

A See and Say

The Spelling Concept

form + al = formal   *adjective* Proper, not casual

form + ality = formality   *noun* Quality of being formal

trans + form = transform   *verb* To make a great change

Many new words are formed by adding prefixes and suffixes and other word endings to the base word *form*, which means "a type or kind of shape." These words may represent different parts of speech, but they are related in spelling and meaning.

B Link Sounds and Letters

Say each spelling word. Look for the base word *form* in each word. Then sort all the words except the first one on a chart like this.

You can look up a formula.

MEMORY JOGGER

Word Sort		
____ form	____ form ____	form ____

C Write and Check

Complete the word chains below. In each sentence, the second and third *form* words have more word parts than the first *form* word.

1. To form a formula, we need to find useful

_ _ _ _ _ _ _ _ _ _ .

2. Our formal uniforms create an air of _ _ _ _ _ _ _ _ .

Now use other spelling words to write your own word chain.

_____

_____

A Build Vocabulary: Word Families

A word family is a series of related words. The words share the same base word or root, but their meanings, spellings, and parts of speech vary.

Form a spelling word for each item below.

1. base word + *al*

2. *in* + base word + *al*

3. *re* + base word + *ing*

4. *un* + *in* + base word + *ed*

5. *in* + base word + *ative*

6. *in* + base word + *ation* + *al*

7. base word + *less*

8. *in* + base word + *al* + *ly*

Spell Chat
With a partner, brainstorm as many other words as you can that contain the word **form**, such as *conformist* and *formally*.

B Word Study: Nouns and Verbs

A noun is a word that names a person, place, or thing. A verb is a word that expresses an action or state of being. For each sentence below, write a noun or verb from the spelling list.

9. The president's actions are _____ to her beliefs.

10. That tadpole will _____ itself into a frog.

11. Please _____ a line behind Jason.

12. My little brother wears his team _____ to bed!

13. Please _____ to the rules.

14. The lawyer will _____ you about your legal rights.

15. I watched his _____ from a poor student to a fine one.

16. The presidential inauguration is an occasion of great _____.

17. I like the appearance, or _____, of the newspaper.

18. What is the _____ for that chemical compound?

19. This _____ will help you research the report.

20. He promises to _____ and change his poor behavior.

Be a Spelling Sleuth

Look for words in the form family. You'll find them in nonfiction books and articles about computers and the information superhighway. Keep a list of the words you find.

Spelling Words

form	informally
formal	information
informal	informational
formality	informative
formula	uninformed
formless	reform
format	reforming
conform	uniform
conforming	transform
inform	transformation

LOOKOUT WORD

Review	Challenge
terrarium	misinform
volcanoes	misinformation
performance	

My Words

_____

_____

_____

Spelling Words

form	informally
formal	information
informal	informational
formality	informative
formula	uninformed
formless	reform
format	reforming
conform	uniform
conforming	transform
inform	transformation

Review	Challenge
terrarium	misinform
volcanoes	misinformation
performance	

My Words

_____
_____
_____

Quick Write

Write two or three sentences you would use in a speech if you ran for student president of your school. Include words with form in them.

A Write an Article

You may wish to do this activity on a computer.

The mayor of your community has asked you and your classmates to suggest ways to improve the life of people your age. Write a short article summarizing a meeting between the students and the mayor of your community. Use your spelling words; also use adjectives and adverbs to make your writing more colorful.

B Proofread

Read the opening of Kurt's article. Correct four spelling errors, two errors with adverbs and adjectives, and one other error.

Tip

Adjectives and adverbs are describing words. Adjectives describe nouns; adverbs describe verbs, adjectives, and other adverbs. Adverbs frequently end in *ly*.

Last Thursday, the mayor held an infomative meeting. He invited sixth-grade students to an informel meeting to express their views about the future of Jamesburg. The students' ideas were well thought out and clear expressed.

One student, Tanya Williams, proposed that the mayor appoint a sixth grader to represent the voice of youth at monthly town council meetings. The performence of the youths at the meeting showed their excellently preparation. Now no one is uniformed about students' views.

Now proofread your article. Check your spelling, punctuation, and grammar.

PROOFREADING MARKS

∧ Add
⅄ Add a comma
ᱯ ᱰ Add quotation marks
⊙ Add a period
ℓ Take out
ᴑᴧ Move
≡ Capital letter
/ Small letter
¶ Indent

A Use the Dictionary: Stressed Syllables

Look at the entry word and pronunciation for *transform*. The pronunciation shows how to pronounce the word. The syllable that is pronounced with more stress is in boldfaced type. Some dictionaries use a stress mark to show the stressed syllable.

trans•form /trans fôrm/ *verb* To make a great change in something. *Learning a second language has transformed my life.*
▷ **transforming, transformed** *noun* **transformation**

Write the words below in syllables. Then say each word and circle the syllable that should get the greater stress. If necessary, use your Spelling Dictionary for help.

- formula _____
- formality _____
- informative _____

B Test Yourself

Look at the pronunciation for each spelling word below. Pronounce each word. Then write it.

1. in **fôr** məl
2. **fôr** myə lə
3. in **fôrm**
4. **fôrm** lis
5. **fôr** məl
6. **fôrm**
7. in fər **mā** shən əl
8. **fôr** mat
9. in fər **mā** shən
10. **fôr mal** i tē
11. in **fôr** mə tiv
12. in **fôr** məl ē
13. ri **fôrm** ing
14. un in **fôrmd**
15. ri **fôrm**
16. yōō nə **fôrm**
17. kən **fôrm**
18. trans **fôrm**
19. kən **fôr** ming
20. trans fər **mā** shən

For Tomorrow...
Get ready to share the **form** words you discovered in publications about computers and the information superhighway. Remember to study for the test!

Get Word Wise

If the word *form* means "a shape," what does it mean to be an *informer*? The prefix *in-* here means "toward," and the suffix *-er* means "one who." So an informer is "one who shapes an idea and sends it toward someone or something else."

Word Study Strategy

See the word

Say it slowly

Link sounds and letters

Write

Check

END

Spelling Words

unity
union
reunion
unite
unison
unicorn
unicycle
universe
universal
university
unique *LOOKOUT WORD*
decade
decimal
century
centimeter
centipede
centennial
centigrade
percent
percentage

Review	Challenge
formula	decathlon
population	unanimous
monogram	

My Words

_____

_____

_____

Number Prefixes and Roots

A See and Say

The Spelling Concept

uni + cycle = unicycle a bicycle with one wheel and no handlebars

dec + imal = decimal a number based on multiples of ten

cent + ury = century a period of 100 years

Many English words contain prefixes, roots, and other word parts that mean numbers. For example, *uni* from the Latin word *unus* means "one," *dec* from the Greek word *deka* means "ten," and c*ent* from the Latin word c*entum* means "a hundred."

Pete and Pam wore **uni**forms and rode their **uni**cycles at the reunion.

MEMORY JOGGER

B Link Sounds and Letters

Say each spelling word. Listen for the word part that relates to a number. Then write the words in the correct column on a chart like the one below.

Word Sort

uni	dec	cent

C Write and Check

Can you answer this riddle with two of your spelling words? Then write a riddle of your own that uses two spelling words for an answer.

_____

_____

_____

RIDDLE
Where would you go to learn how to ride a one-wheeled cycle?

unicycle university

A Build Vocabulary: **Word Meanings**

Write the spelling word that fits each definition below. Use the Spelling Dictionary if you need help.

1. ten groups of ten years
2. one-hundredth of a meter
3. a hundred-legged creature
4. a one-hundred-year celebration
5. a measurement of temperature at which water boils at 100 degrees
6. the state of being one or united
7. the joining together of two or more things to form one larger group
8. to join together, as one
9. people doing the same thing at the same time
10. an imaginary one-horned creature
11. a one-wheeled riding device
12. all that exists, including the earth and space
13. shared by everyone and everything
14. all the colleges on a campus
15. one of a kind

B Word Study: **Prefixes and Roots**

Write the spelling word for each definition below.

16. a meeting of people again after a long time apart
17. a ten-year period
18. a number system that has ten as its base
19. a part that is one one-hundredth
20. a fraction or proportion of something expressed as a number out of a hundred

Be a Spelling Sleuth

Be on the lookout in sports magazines for words that have number prefixes and roots. Make a list of the words you find.

Spell Chat

Challenge the person next to you to suggest two other words that contain *uni, dec,* or *cent.*

Spelling Words	
unity	unique
union	decade
reunion	decimal
unite	century
unison	centimeter
unicorn	centipede
unicycle	centennial
universe	centigrade
universal	percent
university	percentage

Review	Challenge
formula	decathlon
population	unanimous
monogram	

My Words

_____

_____

_____

Spelling Words

unity	unique
union	decade
reunion	decimal
unite	century
unison	centimeter
unicorn	centipede
unicycle	centennial
universe	centigrade
universal	percent
university	percentage

LOOKOUT WORD

Review	Challenge
formula	decathlon
population	unanimous
monogram	

My Words

_____
_____
_____

Quick Write

Write three sentences about an important event that you remember from the past. Use as many words with number prefixes and roots as you can.

A Write Historical Fiction

 You may wish to do this activity on a computer.

Choose an event from history that you know something about. Create a fictional incident to add to the event. Write the opening of a historical fiction narrative in which you set the scene and introduce your subject. Include several spelling words, and try to use compound sentences with conjunctions such as *and*, *or*, and *but*.

B Proofread

Read Michael's opening to his narrative about a historical event into which he introduces a fictional element. He made four spelling errors, two punctuation errors, and two capitalization errors. Correct them.

Tip
Be sure to use a comma before the conjunction in a compound sentence.

> It is the first Tuesday in November, 1960 and the adult populashun of the United States is lining up at the polls. Voters do this two or three times a deckade to elect a President This time they will cast a vote either for John F. Kennedy, a Democrat from massachusetts, or Richard M. Nixon, a republican from California.
>
> As the sun finally breaks through the afternoon clouds, Louis Karash, an elderly man in the crowd, explains to his granddaughter that voting is a uneque opportunity to participate in the future of the Unoin.

Now proofread your own work of historical fiction. Check your spelling, grammar, punctuation, and capitalization.

PROOFREADING MARKS

∧	Add
⩔	Add a comma
⌄⌄	Add quotation marks
⊙	Add a period
ℓ	Take out
⟳	Move
≡	Capital letter
/	Small letter
¢	Indent

A Use the Dictionary: Guide Words

You can use the two guide words at the top of each dictionary page to help you find words quickly. The word at the left is the first word defined on that page; the word at the right is the last word found on the page. Look at the guide words on the dictionary page below. The word *percent* can be found on this page.

> **penitentiary ▶ perch**
>
> **per·cent** /pər sent/ *noun*
>
> **1.** One part of a hundred, written using the symbol %. *A quarter is 25% of one dollar.*

Assume that the two words below are guide words on a dictionary page. Write nine spelling words from this lesson that you would find on this page.

unicycle ▶ unknown

_____

_____

B Test Yourself

Write the spelling words in alphabetical order. To do this correctly, you may have to look beyond the third and fourth letter.

For Tomorrow...
Get ready to share the words you found
with **number prefixes** and
roots.
Remember to study for
your test!

Get Word Wise

The word *centipede* comes from the Latin roots *centum*, which means "hundred," and *ped*, meaning "foot." Centipedes have one pair of legs attached to each section of their bodies. Certain centipedes more than live up to their names. Some have as many as 170 pairs of legs!

Word Study Strategy

See the word

Say it slowly

Link sounds and letters

Write

Check

END

Spelling Words

fact
factual
factor
factory
manufacture
manufacturer
artifact
artificial
benefit
beneficial
perfect
perfection
effect
effective
infection
infectious *LOOKOUT WORD*
satisfaction
satisfactory
dissatisfaction
unsatisfactory

Review	Challenge
unique	facsimile
overwhelmed	fax
official	

My Words

_____
_____
_____

Words With the Latin Roots fac, fic

Ⓐ See and Say

The Spelling Concept

beneficial	having a good effect
manufacture	to make or produce something

The Latin roots *fac* and *fic* mean "to make" or "to do." The root *fac* is sometimes spelled as *fec*, and the root *fic* sometimes appears as *fit* in English. Suffixes and other word parts are often joined to these Latin roots to make a large number of English words.

The best medicine is effective.

MEMORY JOGGER

Ⓑ Link Sounds and Letters

Say each spelling word. Listen for the different sounds of the roots *fac* and *fic*. Then write the spelling words on a chart like the one below.

Word Sort

fic	fec	fac	fit

Ⓒ Write and Check

Say this tongue twister aloud. How fast can you go? Write the spelling words you found in the tongue twister.

_____

Now write your own tongue twister, using as many words with the Latin roots *fac* and *fic* as you can.

_____

_____

TONGUE TWISTER

Can you find a factor in the math fact factory?

A Build Vocabulary: Roots

In each of the following word groups, the Latin root *fac* is spelled *fec*. Write the spelling words that are related to each word group. The last letter of each spelling word is given as a clue.

infect, infecting

1. _____ n

2. _____ s

perfectly, perfectible

3. _____ t

4. _____ n

effectively, effectiveness

5. _____ t

6. _____ e

B Word Study: Word Meanings

For each definition below, write the appropriate spelling word.

7. information that is proven to be true

8. relating to something that is true

9. one of the things that produces a result

10. a place where things are made, often using machines

11. to make or produce with machines

12. a person or company involved with making things with machines

13. an object made by human beings

14. the state of being satisfied

15. good enough but not outstanding

16. to get an advantage from or to be helped by something

17. having a good effect; helpful

18. not natural

19. the state of being unhappy or discontented

20. not good enough

Be a Spelling Sleuth

Check science fiction books and magazines as well as movie posters for words with the Latin roots fac and fic. Make a list of all the words you find.

Spell Chat

Challenge the person next to you to choose a spelling word, identify the root, and name other words with the same root.

Spelling Words

fact	perfect
factual	perfection
factor	effect
factory	effective
manufacture	infection
manufacturer	infectious
artifact	satisfaction
artificial	satisfactory
benefit	dissatisfaction
beneficial	unsatisfactory

Review	Challenge
unique	facsimile
overwhelmed	fax
official	

My Words

_____

_____

_____

Write and Proofread

Spelling Words

fact	perfect
factual	perfection
factor	effect
factory	effective
manufacture	infection
manufacturer	infectious (LOOKOUT WORD)
artifact	satisfaction
artificial	satisfactory
benefit	dissatisfaction
beneficial	unsatisfactory

Review	Challenge
unique	facsimile
overwhelmed	fax
official	

My Words

Quick Write

Write three sentences that might be used in advertisements for products you are familiar with. Use as many words with the roots fac and fic as you can.

A Write Information for a Brochure

You may wish to do this activity on a computer.

You own a large manufacturing company, and you're about to launch a new product. What is special about the product you make? Write information for a brochure to persuade someone to buy your product. Use words with the Latin roots *fac* and *fic*. Make sure to indent the first line of each paragraph.

B Proofread

Tip
Indent the first line of each paragraph you write.

Read this section from Marianne's brochure. She made five spelling errors, one punctuation error, one paragraph indentation error, and one capitalization error. Correct the errors.

Tennis Buddy is an affective system that allows you to practice tennis by yourself. What makes Tennis Buddy so benefitial. we manufachure it using a unique design. The affect of this design is a system that sends practice balls to the player at regular intervals. Use the brand that professional tennis players have made their offitial practice partner—Tennis Buddy.

PROOFREADING MARKS

- ∧ Add
- ∧ Add a comma
- " " Add quotation marks
- ⊙ Add a period
- Take out
- Move
- ≡ Capital letter
- / Small letter
- ¶ Indent

Now proofread your own section of a brochure. Check your spelling, grammar, punctuation, capitalization, and paragraph indentations.

A Use the Dictionary: Multiple Meanings

Many words have more than one meaning. The dictionary lists the different meanings of a word and numbers them. Here is a dictionary entry for the word *factor*. How do the example sentences help you to understand the two different meanings of the word?

> **fac·tor** /fak tər/ *noun*
>
> **1.** Something that helps produce a result. *Randy's new training schedule was a factor in his winning the race.* **2.** A whole number that can be divided exactly into a larger number. *The numbers 1, 2, 3, 4, 6, and 12 are factors of 12.*

Now write two of your own sentences with *factor*. Use a different meaning of the word in each sentence.

B Test Yourself

Write the spelling word that solves each of the following word puzzles. The symbol ❑ stands for the letters *fac* or *fec*. The symbol * stands for the letters *fic* or *fit*.

1. manu❑turer
2. bene*
3. in❑tion
4. arti❑t
5. per❑t
6. bene*ial
7. manu❑ture
8. per❑tion
9. ef❑tive
10. ❑tory
11. satis❑tion
12. ef❑t
13. satis❑tory
14. dissatis❑tion
15. arti*ial
16. unsatis❑tory
17. ❑tual
18. in❑tious
19. ❑tor
20. ❑t

For Tomorrow...
Get ready to share the words that you found with the Latin roots **fac** and **fic**. Remember to study for your test!

Get Word Wise

The Latin root **fac** means "to do" or "to make." *Manu* comes from the Latin root *manus*, which means "a hand." The meaning of *manufacture* has developed over time from "things made by hand" to "things made by physical labor, especially with machines."

Word Study Strategy

See the word

Say it slowly

Link sounds and letters

Write

Check

END

Spelling Words

brunch
sitcom
moped   LOOKOUT WORD
twirl
meld
modem
motel
motorcade
slosh
smash
smog
splatter
squiggle
squinch
tangelo
taxicab
laser
radar
scuba
infomercial

Review	Challenge
infectious	telethon
explanation	Internet
nuclear	

My Words

_____
_____
_____

Invented Words

A See and Say

The Spelling Concept

brunch = breakfast + lunch
radar = radio detecting and ranging

Many words in English are invented words. An invented word is often formed by blending two English words into one. Acronyms are invented words formed from the first letters or syllables of a series of words.

First take a **SQUI**rm and then take a wri**GGLE**. Add them up and make a **SQUIGGLE**!

MEMORY JOGGER

B Link Sounds and Letters

Say each spelling word. Listen carefully to the number of syllables in each word. Then sort the spelling words on a chart like the one below.

Word Sort

One Syllable	Two Syllables	Three Syllables	Four Syllables

C Write and Check

The answer to this riddle contains one of your spelling words. Can you figure it out? Write the spelling word below. Then write another riddle with an answer that contains another spelling word.

_____
_____
_____
_____

RIDDLE
What's worse than raining cats and dogs?
hailing taxicabs

A Build Vocabulary: Invented Words

Invented words are often formed by blending parts of two English words into one. Write the spelling word that completes each equation.

1. modulator + demodulator =
2. taximeter + cabriolet =
3. twist + whirl =
4. squint + pinch =
5. melt + weld =
6. motor + hotel =
7. smoke + fog =
8. motor + pedal =
9. splash + spatter =
10. information + commercial =
11. squirm + wriggle =
12. smack + mash =
13. slop + slush =
14. breakfast + lunch =
15. motor + cavalcade =
16. tangerine + pomelo =
    (*Pomelo* is another word for *grapefruit*.)
17. situation + comedy =

B Word Study: Acronyms

Acronyms are formed from the first letters or syllables of a series of words. Use the first letters or syllables in the equations below to form spelling words.

18. *se*lf-contained + *u*nderwater + *b*reathing + *a*pparatus =
19. *ra*dio + *d*etecting + *a*nd + *r*anging =
20. *l*ight + *a*mplification by + *s*timulated + *e*mission of + *r*adiation =

Spell Chat

Challenge a classmate to use another acronym, such as *NASA* or *NATO*, in an original sentence.

Be a Spelling Sleuth

Acronyms and invented words provide a shorter way to say something. List invented words and acronyms that you find in newspapers and science magazines, words such as skylab (sky laboratory) and zip (zone improvement plan) code.

Spelling Words

brunch	smog
sitcom	splatter
moped	squiggle
twirl	squinch
meld	tangelo
modem	taxicab
motel	laser
motorcade	radar
slosh	scuba
smash	infomercial

LOOKOUT WORD

Review	Challenge
infectious	telethon
explanation	Internet
nuclear	

My Words

_____

_____

_____

Spelling Words

brunch	smog
sitcom	splatter
moped *LOOKOUT WORD*	squiggle
twirl	squinch
meld	tangelo
modem	taxicab
motel	laser
motorcade	radar
slosh	scuba
smash	infomercial

Review	Challenge
infectious	telethon
explanation	Internet
nuclear	

My Words

_____

_____

_____

Quick Write

Use three spelling words from this lesson in the lead sentence of a newspaper article about a public official. Include spelling words like *motorcade* and *brunch*.

A Write an Informative Article

You may choose to do this activity on a computer.

You have signed up as a tutor for a younger student in your school. Write a brief article explaining how you plan to help the student. Use a variety of verbs to convey the action.

B Proofread

Proofread Nina's informative article. She made five spelling errors, one capitalization error, and one grammar error with verbs. Correct them.

Tip
Remember that -ed is added to most verbs to show past time.

> I am going to help a second-grader from israel with English. When I first met Mina, I noticed her infektious laugh and her squigle. I will help her sit still, listen to my explainations, and encourage her to talk to me in English. We will also "talk" by modim on our computers. I plan to invite her to my family's brench so she can practice speaking English. I have want to help tutor someone for a long time now.

Now proofread your informative article. Check spelling, grammar, punctuation, capitalization, and verb forms.

PROOFREADING MARKS

∧	Add
⌄	Add a comma
⌄⌄	Add quotation marks
⊙	Add a period
ℓ	Take out
↶↷	Move
≡	Capital letter
/	Small letter
¶	Indent

A Use the Dictionary: Entry Words

Dictionaries usually don't define every form of a word in a separate entry. Here's a dictionary entry for the verb *splatter*. Notice how additional forms are listed at the end without definitions. From the given definition, you can figure out that the noun form must mean "the act or sound of splashing with drops."

splat•ter /splat ər/ *verb*

To splash with drops. ▷ *verb* **splatters, splattering, splattered** ▷ *noun* **splatter**

Write three short sentences, using three of the four forms of *splatter* that are listed at the end of the dictionary entry above.

B Test Yourself

Each word or term below is part of an invented word from this lesson. Write the spelling word that is derived from each numbered item.

1. breathing apparatus
2. hotel
3. breakfast
4. taximeter
5. twist
6. radio detecting
7. light amplification
8. comedy
9. tangerine
10. wriggle
11. pedal
12. spatter
13. weld
14. slop
15. modulator
16. pinch
17. cavalcade
18. smack
19. smoke
20. commercial

For Tomorrow...
Be ready to share your list of acronyms and invented words. Remember to study for your test!

Get Word Wise

Acronyms and invented words are made up as they are needed. In 1905, smoke from a growing number of factories mixed with fog, causing air pollution. People began calling the dirty air smog.

Word Study Strategy

See the word

Say it slowly

Link sounds and letters

Write

Check

END

Internet Fever

Write words from the box to complete the paragraphs.

transformation	infectious	unique
beneficial	information	

Excitement about the possibilities of the Internet seems to be **(1)** these days. Everyone wants to log on. The **(2)** caused by the Internet has been amazing. Once used only by university professors and government scientists, today the Internet has become a **(3)** tool for many different people. The World Wide Web contains pictures and sounds as well as text. This part of the Internet offers a **(4)** opportunity for people from around the world to exchange **(5)** and pictures with one another.

infomercial	terrain	percentage	informative

To find your way around the virtual landscape or **(6)** , it may be helpful to watch an **(7)** , which can show you the best way to locate what you want on the Web. You can visit a Web site to hear the latest songs, read a review of the latest hit movie, or find out the statistics for last night's game. There are many **(8)** and interesting Web sites, but it could take years to explore the entire Internet on your own. In the meantime, enjoy the **(9)** of sites that you do visit.

factual	formula	universe
earthshaking	artifact	earthbound

There is no exact **(10)** for using the Internet. Have fun and roam around, even if you are looking for specific, **(11)** information. You never know what you may find. Once, I logged on to search for a report on an ancient Egyptian **(12)** . I found what I was looking for, but not before I saw a video of a trip down the Nile River. Next, I think I'll visit the World Wide Web site for outer space and explore the **(13)** from my desk chair. We may be **(14)** , but with the help of modern technology, we can have **(15)** experiences.

What on Earth?

Write the Review Word that answers each question about what's happening on the earth.

1. Who studies rocks on the earth? _____

2. What do we call the study of the earth, including its people, resources, climate, and physical features? _____

3. What is a glass-encased planter with plants in soil called?

   _____

4. What do we call a violent shaking of the earth? _____

5. What is a name for a dog that is a good digger? _____

6. What branch of mathematics studies the lines, angles, and shapes found on the earth? _____

7. What kinds of claims did France make to land in the Old Northwest Territory? _____

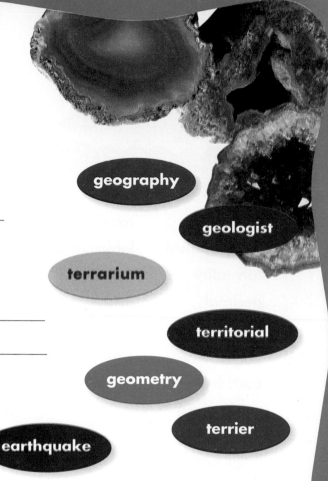

geography

geologist

terrarium

territorial

geometry

terrier

earthquake

Word Invention

Fill each blank with a Review Word.

| radar | modem | brunch | tangelo |
| sitcom | smog | splatter | motel |

8. For _____ at my favorite restaurant, I will begin with a _____ .

9. The police use _____ to identify speeding cars near the _____ .

10. The TV _____ joked about snow in the East and _____ in the West.

11. Try not to _____ your apple juice on my computer _____ .

TRY THIS

Start with the base word *fact*. Write four other Review Words that contain this base word.

_____

_____

_____

_____

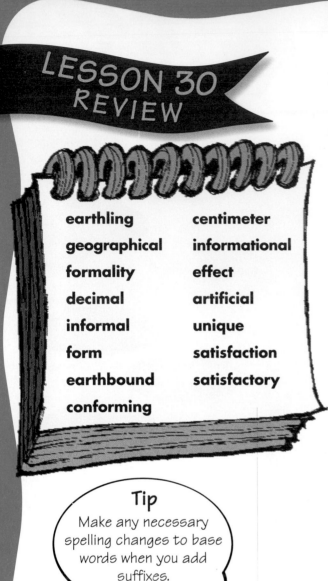

earthling
geographical
formality
decimal
informal
form
earthbound
conforming

centimeter
informational
effect
artificial
unique
satisfaction
satisfactory

Tip

Make any necessary spelling changes to base words when you add suffixes.

Field Notes in Camp

Whether you are going on a camping trip or on a photo safari, taking field notes will help you remember what you do and see. Field notes provide a brief account of each day. Write two field notes about what you see and do each day of an imaginary four-day trip. Make sure you use each of the boxed Review Words at least once in your notes.

Day 1
1. _____
2. _____

Day 2
3. _____
4. _____

Day 3
5. _____
6. _____

Day 4
7. _____
8. _____

Look back at the words you misspelled in your Unit 5 Posttests. Use them to write additional field notes.

Tell About It

Choose one of the field notes, and expand it to write a postcard to a friend about your trip. Proofread your postcard for spelling, punctuation, grammar, and capitalization.

_____

_____

_____

_____

_____

_____

_____

PROOFREADING MARKS

∧ Add
⋏ Add a comma
⌄⌄ Add quotation marks
⊙ Add a period
ℓ Take out
↶↷ Move
≡ Capital letter
/ Small letter
¶ Indent

Number Prefixes and Roots

You can find out what a book is about by reading the description on the book jacket. Choose the correct word to complete each of the following book descriptions.

unicycle   unicorn

1. In *Wonders of the Past,* you'll delight in tales of the legendary

_____ and discover ancient diagrams such as a

sketch for the first _____ .

reunion   unison

2. In *All-Star Comeback,* the _____ of the 1986

NBA champion Los Angeles Lakers ends in a game with the

present-day players. In _____ , appreciative fans

cheer for the teams. You'll be surprised how the game ends.

formula   uniform

3. *Strike Up the Band* follows the day-to-day life of a high school

band member. From finding a(n) _____ that

fits to practicing the school song, Teresa enjoys being a band

member. She thinks of the band as her _____

for success. She hopes to get a music scholarship for college.

centennial   centigrade

4. *Celebration on Ice* provides a hilarious account of how a town's

_____ celebration goes sour. Everyone thought

a parade on ice would be great, but no one thought about

what would happen if the water temperature rose above

0° on a _____ scale!

Tasha says...

My dog, Terry, is unique. Last year she vanished from our yard. I made lost-dog signs and posted them around town. Next to her picture, I wrote, "Have you seen this unique terror on the loose?" A man who had seen my dog called, but he was afraid to go near her. I told him that she's friendly. "You said she was a terror," he protested. I groaned, "She's a *terrier*." Luckily, he still knew where she was. Next time I think I'll check my spelling more carefully.

Spelling Matters!

LESSON 31

Spelling Words

timely
untimely
timeless
timeworn
timepiece
timetable
daytime
summertime
springtime
wintertime
timekeeper
timesaver
time-out LOOKOUT WORD
tempo
temporary
temporarily
contemporary
chronicle LOOKOUT WORD
chronic
chronological

Review	Challenge
moped	synchronize
extensive	untimeliness
journal	

My Words

_____

_____

_____

"Time" Words

A See and Say

The Spelling Concept

time	+	table	=	timetable
time	+	less	=	timeless
temp	+	orary	=	temporary
chron	+	ic	=	chronic

The base word *time* is found in compound words and in words with prefixes and suffixes. The Latin root *temp* and the Greek root *chron* also mean "time."

What is the **tempo** of con**tempo**rary life?

MEMORY JOGGER

B Link Sounds and Letters

Say each spelling word, and listen for the base word or root that means "time." Then write your spelling words in a chart like the one below.

Word Sort

Words With time	Words With temp	Words With chron

C Write and Check

Complete the word puzzle below.

What's the opposite of *permanently*? _ _ _ _ _ _ _ _ _ _ _ .

If you change the word into an adjective, it becomes: _ _ _ _ _ _ _ _ _ . If you change it to a noun and add a musical beat, it becomes _ _ _ _ _ .

Now write a sentence describing something that is permanent and another sentence about something that is temporary.

_____

_____

A Build Vocabulary: Analogies

An analogy shows a similarity between pairs of things. Complete each sentence below with the spelling word that makes the second pair of words similar to the first. Write each spelling word.

1. *Dark* is to *nighttime* as *light* is to _____

2. *Car* is to *vehicle* as *wristwatch* is to _____

3. *Falling leaves* are to *autumn* as *new blossoms* are to _____

4. *Young* is to *fresh* as *old* is to _____

5. *Price* is to *priceless* as *time* is to _____

6. *Movie* is to *movie schedule* as *train* is to _____

7. *Hot* is to *summertime* as *cold* is to _____

8. *Short days* are to *wintertime* as *long days* are to _____

B Word Study: Roots and Base Words

Complete each sentence with a spelling word that contains the root or base shown.

9. (temp) The song will take less time if you increase the _____.

10. (chron) Kit has a _____ illness.

11. (temp) Was Anne Hathaway a _____ of Shakespeare?

12. (time) The _____ signaled the end of the game.

13. (chron) A diary is like a _____ of a person's life.

14. (temp) Are you living here permanently or just _____?

15. (time) The coach called for a _____ in the first quarter.

16. (chron) The plot of most stories unfolds in _____ order.

17. (temp) A pencil leaves a _____ mark, not a permanent one.

18. (time) Many people use a microwave oven as a _____.

C Write

Write two "time" spelling words that are antonyms ending in *-ly.*

_____

Be a Spelling Sleuth

Look for "time" words in schedules of all kinds—bus or train schedules and class schedules. Also check cookbooks for words related to time. Keep a list of the words you find.

Spell Chat

With a classmate, make up phrases, using the spelling words. Examples are *a timely decision* and *temporarily broken.*

Spelling Words

timely	timekeeper
untimely	timesaver
timeless	time-out `LOOKOUT WORD`
timeworn	tempo
timepiece	temporary
timetable	temporarily
daytime	contemporary
summertime	chronicle `LOOKOUT WORD`
springtime	chronic
wintertime	chronological

Review	Challenge
moped	synchronize
extensive	untimeliness
journal	

My Words

_____

_____

_____

Spelling Words

timely	timekeeper
untimely	timesaver
timeless	time-out LOOKOUT WORD
timeworn	tempo
timepiece	temporary
timetable	temporarily
daytime	contemporary
summertime	chronicle LOOKOUT WORD
springtime	chronic
wintertime	chronological

Review	Challenge
moped	synchronize
extensive	untimeliness
journal	

My Words

_____

_____

_____

Quick Write ✏️

Write two lines of dialogue with "time" words that a visitor might say while attending a special event at your school. Be sure to use at least one spelling word.

A Write a Conversation

 You may wish to do this activity on a computer.

Imagine that you live in a land where people have to use a "time" word in every sentence they speak. The word can be based on *time, temp,* or *chron,* or it can be any word that refers to time. Write a conversation among several people in this land. Include possessive nouns in your conversation.

B Proofread

Read the conversation that Yolanda wrote. She made four spelling errors, three punctuation errors, and one capitalization error. Correct them.

> **Tip**
> When you write a possessive noun, be sure to use an apostrophe, for example, *Phillip's bicycle.*

"The country of Timetalk has a cronic news shortage," said Mr. Lee. I think I'm going to start publishing an extencive daily news journal."

"Another news chronical would be timely" agreed Ms. Nells.

"Having all the news in one place would be a timesavor," said Mr. Jones. "However, a publishers job requires you to be on call day and night."

"Don't forget," warned ms. Nells. "Morning news is timeworn by lunchtime!"

Now proofread your conversation. Check for correct spelling, capitalization, and punctuation.

PROOFREADING MARKS

∧	Add
⊻	Add a comma
⌄	Add quotation marks
⊙	Add a period
ℓ	Take out
⟳	Move
≡	Capital letter
/	Small letter
¢	Indent

A Use the Dictionary: Guide Words

Guide words show the first and last entry words on a dictionary page. They can help you find entries quickly. The guide words below will help you find the entry for *timetable*. All the entry words on the page fall alphabetically between *timeless* and *Tlingit*.

timeless ▶ Tlingit

Write the three spelling words from this lesson that would have entries on a dictionary page with the following guide words.

temperate ▶ tenant

B Test Yourself

Form the spelling words below by substituting *time, temp,* or *chron* for *time word* and adding word parts.

1. time word+*ly*= _____

2. time word+*o*= _____

3. time word+*less*= _____

4. time word+*ic*= _____

5. time word+*piece*= _____

6. time word+*out*= _____

7. *day*+time word= _____

8. time word+*keeper*= _____

9. *spring*+time word= _____

10. *winter*+time word= _____

11. *un*+time word+*ly*= _____

12. time word+*orary*= _____

13. con+time word+*orary*= _____

14. time word+*worn*= _____

15. *summer*+time word= _____

16. time word+*saver*= _____

17. time word+*table*= _____

18. time word+*icle*= _____

19. time word+*orarily*= _____

20. time word+*ological*= _____

For Tomorrow...
Be prepared to share the **"time" words** you found in schedules and cookbooks. Remember to study for the test!

Get Word Wise

Like many English words about music, *tempo* comes from Italian, a modern language related to Latin. In Italian, *tempo* means not only "time" and "musical timing" but also "weather." How do you think weather and time are related?

Word Study Strategy

See the word

Say it slowly

Link sounds and letters

Write

Check

END

LESSON 32

Spelling Words

chord
chorus
choral
choir LOOKOUT WORD
chemist
chemical
chemistry
chaos
chaotic
chameleon
character
characteristic
anchor
architect
architecture
archive
monarch
monarchy
mechanic
mechanical

Review	Challenge
chronicle	choreography
geology	cholesterol
zucchini	

My Words

_____
_____
_____

Words With ch for /k/

A See and Say

The Spelling Concept

ch orus   mech anic   monarch

In most English words, *ch* has the same sound as in the beginning of *chin* and *chew*. Sometimes, however, *ch* is pronounced /k/. This /k/ can be found at the beginning, middle, or end of a word.

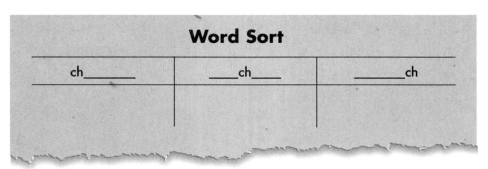

The choir sang a cheerful song.

MEMORY JOGGER

B Link Sounds and Letters

Say each spelling word and listen for /k/. Notice that /k/ is spelled with a *ch*. Now sort your words according to where the *ch* appears in the word, at the beginning, middle, or end. Use a chart like the one below.

Word Sort

ch_____	____ch____	_____ch

C Write and Check

Can you rearrange the letters in each phrase to form a spelling word? Try and solve the puzzles!

What spelling word can you find in "my anchor"?

– – – – – – – –

What spelling word can you find in "Ms. Techi"?

– – – – – – –

Write a sentence, using one of these two spelling words.

_____

_____

A Build Vocabulary: Word Meanings

Read each word meaning below. Write the spelling word it describes.

1. a group of performers who sing _____
2. part of a song repeated after each verse _____
3. one who works on machines _____
4. someone who designs buildings _____
5. the activity of designing buildings _____
6. a lizard that can change color _____
7. a heavy hook _____
8. a government ruled by one person _____
9. one who rules alone like a king _____
10. person in a story _____
11. place where public records are kept _____
12. total confusion _____
13. scientific study of substances _____
14. one who studies chemical substances _____
15. musical notes played at the same time _____

B Adjectives From Nouns

Write the missing adjective in each sentence. Each spelling word is formed from the noun in parentheses.

16. (chorus) The entire class will do a _____ reading of the poem.
17. (chemist) Many new substances are created through _____ research.
18. (chaos) A busy train station is a _____ place.
19. (mechanic) Did the car crash due to _____ failure?
20. (character) One _____ quality of science fiction movies is their use of special effects.

Be a Spelling Sleuth

Look through newspapers, magazines, and classified ads to find words in which ch is pronounced /k/. Make a list of the words you find.

Spell Chat

With a partner, start a conversation using ch words with /k/. Take turns adding spelling words to it. Make the conversation funny: *My mom works in an archive where they keep a pet chameleon.*

Spelling Words

chord	character
chorus	characteristic
choral	anchor
choir (LOOKOUT WORD)	architect
chemist	architecture
chemical	archive
chemistry	monarch
chaos	monarchy
chaotic	mechanic
chameleon	mechanical

Review	Challenge
chronicle	choreography
geology	cholesterol
zucchini	

My Words

_____

_____

_____

Spelling Words

chord	character
chorus	characteristic
choral	anchor
choir	architect
chemist	architecture
chemical	archive
chemistry	monarch
chaos	monarchy
chaotic	mechanic
chameleon	mechanical

choir — LOOKOUT WORD

Review	Challenge
chronicle	choreography
geology	cholesterol
zucchini	

My Words

_____
_____
_____

Quick Write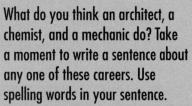

What do you think an architect, a chemist, and a mechanic do? Take a moment to write a sentence about any one of these careers. Use spelling words in your sentence.

You may wish to do this activity on a computer.

Ⓐ Write a Persuasive Paragraph

If your school was holding a career day, which career would you look into? Which careers might interest your classmates? Write a paragraph giving several reasons for someone to choose a particular career. Include spelling words in your reasons.

Ⓑ Proofread

In the paragraph below, André gives his reasons for choosing a career in chemistry. He made four spelling errors, one capitalization error, one grammar error, and two punctuation errors. Correct them.

Tip

When you write three or more items in a series, don't forget to use a comma to separate them. For example, *I could be a doctor, a mechanic, or an architect.*

I became interested in becoming a chemist when I were very young. Both my mother and father were scientists. She was a chemist, and he taught geolagy. They showed me that to be a scientist, you have to be patient curious, and organized. You dont have to be too mecanical, but your lab must be neat. if your lab is messy or kaotic, your experiments could be ruined. Being a chemist is an interesting, exciting job. You may mix a chemicle and end up helping humanity.

PROOFREADING MARKS

∧ Add
⅄ Add a comma
ᵛⱽ Add quotation marks
⊙ Add a period
ℓ Take out
ↄ⌒ Move
≡ Capital letter
╱ Small letter
¶ Indent

Now proofread your persuasive paragraph. Check for correct spelling, grammar, capitalization, and punctuation.

A Use the Dictionary: Multiple Meanings

When words have more than one meaning, dictionaries usually present the different meanings as numbered definitions. For example, the entry below gives three definitions of *character*.

char·ac·ter /kar ik tər/ *noun*

1. The qualities and features of a person or thing that make it different from others.
2. One of the people in a story, book, play, movie, or television program.
3. A letter, figure, or other mark used in printing. *All the letters of the alphabet are characters.*

字 塊 (兒)

Write one context sentence for each of the three different meanings of the word *character*, for example, *It takes a strong character to be a leader* (the first meaning).

_____

_____

_____

B Test Yourself

What letters will complete the spelling words below? Write the words.

1. ch _ _ _
2. ch _ _ _ _ _ _ _
3. ch _ _ _ _
4. _ _ ch _ _
5. ch _ _ _ _ _ _ _ _ _ _ _
6. ch _ _ _ _ _
7. ch _ _ _ _
8. ch _ _ _ _ _ _
9. ch _ _ _ _ _
10. ch _ _ _
11. ch _ _ _ _ _ _
12. ch _ _ _ _ _
13. ch _ _ _
14. _ _ _ _ _ ch _

15. _ _ ch _ _ _ _ _ _ _
16. _ _ ch _ _ _ _ _
17. _ _ _ _ _ ch
18. _ _ ch _ _ _ _
19. _ _ ch _ _ _ _
20. _ _ ch _ _ _

For Tomorrow...
Be ready to share the /k/ words you found in newspapers, magazines, and classified ads. Don't forget to study for the test!

Get Word Wise

The word *archive* comes from the Greek word *archeion*, which means "government house" in the singular and "official documents" in the plural. The National Archives, in Washington, D.C., houses official government documents, including the Declaration of Independence and the Constitution.

Word Study Strategy

See the word

Say it slowly

Link sounds and letters

Write

Check

END

Spelling Words

remember
remembrance
memory
memo
memorial
memorize
memorable
memoir LOOKOUT WORD
memento
communication
common
commonly
uncommon
commonplace
community
communicate
corrupt
disrupt
interrupt
bankrupt

Review	Challenge
choir	memorabilia
informational	bankruptcy
membership	

My Words

_____

_____

_____

Words With the Latin Roots mem, commun, rupt

A See and Say

The Spelling Concept

memory — the power to keep things in mind
community — a group of people who share something in common
disrupt — to break apart; to destroy temporarily

Many English words are formed from Latin roots. The root *commun* means "common or shared." This root is spelled *commun* and *common*. The root *mem* means "remember." The root *rupt* means "break."

Remember that *memoir* comes from French. The letters *oir* are pronounced /wär/.

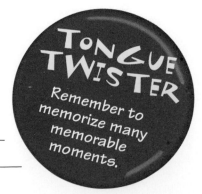

MEMORY JOGGER

B Link Sounds and Letters

Say each spelling word. Look and listen for the root *mem*, *commun*, or *rupt*. Then sort your spelling words on a chart like the one below.

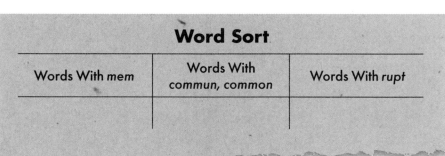

Word Sort

Words With *mem*	Words With *commun, common*	Words With *rupt*

C Write and Check

Say the tongue twister three times. Then write the spelling words you find in the tongue twister. Use some spelling words to write a tongue twister of your own.

_____

_____

_____

TONGUE TWISTER
Remember to memorize many memorable moments.

A Build Vocabulary: Adjectives

Adjectives describe or modify nouns. They tell what kind, how many, or which one. What adjective fits in each blank below? Write the correct spelling word that includes the root in parentheses.

1. (mem) a ___ holiday party
2. (common) a rare orchid of ___ beauty
3. (rupt) a dishonest and ___ politician
4. (mem) a ___ service for soldiers who died in the war
5. (common) a ___ error that many people make
6. (common) a ___ event that happens every day
7. (commun) a ___ gathering place

B Word Study: Roots

Form new words by adding the word parts to each root indicated. Write the correct spelling word.

8. commun + icate
9. commun + ication
10. bank + rupt
11. common + ly
12. dis + rupt
13. inter + rupt
14. mem + oir
15. re + mem + brance
16. mem + ento
17. mem + ory

C Write and Check

Write two sentences, using the words *remember*, *memo*, and *memorize*.

_____

_____

_____

_____

Be a Spelling Sleuth

Be a Spelling Sleuth

Words with the Latin roots mem and commun are common. Look around your school and business *community*. On bulletin boards and store ads, find words related to *communication*. Record these words.

Spell Chat

Challenge a partner to spell three words not on your spelling list with the Latin root **mem**, **commun**, or **rupt**. Then have your partner challenge you to do the same.

Spelling Words

remember	common
remembrance	commonly
memory	uncommon
memo	commonplace
memorial	community
memorize	communicate
memorable	corrupt
memoir	disrupt
memento	interrupt
communication	bankrupt

Review	Challenge
choir	memorabilia
informational	bankruptcy
membership	

My Words

_____

_____

_____

Spelling Words

remember	common
remembrance	commonly
memory	uncommon
memo	commonplace
memorial	community
memorize	communicate
memorable	corrupt
memoir *LOOKOUT WORD*	disrupt
memento	interrupt
communication	bankrupt

Review	Challenge
choir	memorabilia
informational	bankruptcy
membership	

My Words

_____
_____
_____

Quick Write

Write several facts you would include in a memoir about your life. Use as many words as possible with the Latin roots mem, commun, and rupt.

A ## Write a Fable

You may wish to do this activity on a computer.

A fable is a brief story that teaches a lesson. The moral of a fable appears at the end of the fable. Try writing your own fable. Work backwards by writing the moral first.

B ## Proofread

Lena wrote a fable featuring Anansi, the trickster spider in African folklore. Lena made five spelling errors, one error in subject-verb agreement, one punctuation error, and one capitalization error. Correct them.

> **Tip**
> When you write, make sure to use a singular verb with a singular subject and a plural verb with a plural subject.

Anansi wanted the other animals in the jungle community to rimember his name. He demanded that the frogs form a chior to sing his name. He made the monkeys comunicate his name through the language of drums. The birds shouted anansi's name from the skies to make it memorible. The jungle was so noisy that no one could sleep. To this day, the jungle animals thinks of sleepless nights when they hear Anansi's name What is important is not just to be remembered, but to be rembired with fondness.

Now proofread your own fable. Check for spelling, punctuation, and capitalization. Do your subjects and verbs agree?

PROOFREADING MARKS

∧	Add
⋏	Add a comma
＂ ＂	Add quotation marks
⊙	Add a period
ℓ	Take out
⌒	Move
≡	Capital letter
/	Small letter
¶	Indent

A Use the Dictionary: Alphabetizing

In a dictionary, words are presented in alphabetical order, but when words share a root, such as *commun* or *common*, you have to go past the root to alphabetize them. Try it.

com·mon   com·mon·ly   com·mon·place   com·mun·i·cate

Alphabetize these three spelling words: *communicate*, *community*, and *communication*.

_____

_____

_____

Alphabetize these three words with the root *mem*: *memoir*, *memento*, and *memory*.

_____

_____

_____

Alphabetize these four words: *corrupt*, *interrupt*, *disrupt*, and *bankrupt*.

_____

_____

_____

_____

B Test Yourself

When alphabetizing words, you may even need to go to the eleventh letter of a word in order to alphabetize it. For example, *communicate* goes before *communication*. Now write all your spelling words in alphabetical order.

For Tomorrow...
Get ready to share the words with the Latin roots **mem, commun,** and **rupt** that you found on bulletin boards. Don't forget to study for the test!

Get Word Wise

Latin is the parent language of French, Spanish, and Italian. Read the words that mean "community" in those languages.
French = *communauté*
Spanish = *comunidad*
Italian = *comunitá*
What do these words have in common?
(They share the same root, commun.)

Word Study Strategy

See the word

Say it slowly

Link sounds and letters

Write

Check

END

Word Families

A See and Say

The Spelling Concept

create + -ive = creative   creative + -ity = creativity

create + -ion = creation   re- + creation = recreation

You can add prefixes and suffixes to base words to create different words in a word family. Words with the same base are related in spelling and meaning.

Do not think ill of the illustration.

MEMORY JOGGER

B Link Sounds and Letters

Say each group of related spelling words. Listen for the base word in each word family. Then sort the words into five word families on a chart like this one.

Word Sort

create	equal	image	luster	vary

C Write and Check

Imagination has been defined as the ability to *imagine* things you have not experienced. Write a definition for one spelling word that contains another spelling word in the same word family.

_____

_____

_____

_____

A Build Vocabulary: Parts of Speech

Words in a word family are often different parts of speech. Read each incomplete sentence below. Then write the missing spelling word that is the part of speech shown.

1. Look at the __noun__ on that polished car!

2. To solve that math problem, you must use an __noun__ .

3. Can you __verb__ what it would be like to be a rock star?

4. Writing novels requires a good __noun__ .

5. Marcie is very __adjective__ and is always coming up with new ideas.

6. The clever young woman came up with a __adjective__ solution to the problem.

7. For __noun__ , Kim likes to play basketball.

8. That artist can __verb__ a lifelike sculpture.

9. The recipe says to mix __adjective__ portions of flour and water.

10. My little sister has an __adjective__ friend that only she can see.

11. The imaginative dishes Mel prepares show his __noun__ .

12. In the decathlon, athletes perform __adjective__ sports.

13. On open-ended test questions, answers will __verb__ .

14. Will you __verb__ your report with photos or drawings?

B Word Study: Singular and Plural Nouns

A noun names a person, place, or thing. To make a singular noun plural, usually you add *s* to the end of the word. If the noun ends in *y*, you change the *y* to *i* and add *es*. Write the singular form of each plural noun below.

15. illustrations

16. images

17. creations

18. variations

19. varieties

20. variables

Spell Chat

Challenge the person next to you to suggest other words in the *create* word family.

Spelling Words

luster	create
illustrate	creative
illustration	creativity
equal	creation
equation	recreation
image	vary
imagine	variation
imagination	various
imaginary	variety
imaginative	variable

Review	Challenge
memoir	recreational
unity	invariably
cleanliness	

My Words

_____
_____
_____
_____

Spelling Words

luster	create
illustrate	creative
illustration	creativity
equal	creation
equation	recreation
image	vary
imagine	variation
imagination	various
imaginary	variety
imaginative	variable LOOKOUT WORD

Review	Challenge
memoir	recreational
unity	invariably
cleanliness	

My Words

_____

_____

_____

Quick Write

Literature is filled with imaginary places. Write a few sentences describing an imaginary place you have read about or create one of your own. Be sure to use at least one spelling word.

A Write a How-To Guide

You may wish to do this activity on a computer.

Think of yourself as the president of a new club. What is the club's goal? For example, the goal might be to publish a magazine or to create a mural. Write the first four steps that tell how to achieve your goal. Include some of your spelling words.

B Proofread

Here are the four steps that Benita wrote for her how-to guide. She made four spelling errors, two punctuation errors, and one capitalization error. Correct them.

> **Tip**
> Use a comma after an introductory word, such as *first* or *next*, at the beginning of a sentence.

How to put Together a School Magazine

First, publicize the magazine so that people submit lots of possible selections. You may want to hold a contest to encourage people to submit literature. Second look for vareity. A good issue should contain nonfiction, as well as fiction and poetry. The memior, autobiography, and biography are good examples of nonfiction. Third, choose imaginitive works that show creativety on the part of the writers. Last but not least, include creative images to illustrate the writing you select

Now proofread your how-to guide. Check for correct spelling, grammar, capitalization, and punctuation.

PROOFREADING MARKS

∧	Add
⅋	Add a comma
⅋ ⅋	Add quotation marks
⊙	Add a period
ℓ	Take out
○∧	Move
≡	Capital letter
/	Small letter
¢	Indent

A Use the Dictionary: Pronunciation

The correct pronunciation follows each entry word in the dictionary. To understand the pronunciation symbols, look at the pronunciation key. For example, the pronunciation key on page 183 in the Spelling Dictionary tells you that the letter *a* in *variety* is pronounced like the *a* in *above*. Some dictionaries place a pronunciation key on each pair of facing pages. Others have the key in the front or back of the dictionary.

> **va•ri•ety** /və rī i tē/ *noun*
>
> **1.** Difference or change. *My little brother eats only burgers; there is no variety in his diet.* **2.** A selection of different things. **3.** A different type of the same thing, as in *a new variety of rose.* ▷ *plural* **varieties**

Say each spelling word that is respelled below. Then write the spelling word. Use the pronunciation key to help you.

/i **maj** in/ = _____

/krē **ā** shən/ = _____

B Test Yourself

Use the initial and end letter clues to find the spelling words to complete each sentence below. Then write the words.

A person who is c__1__e has a good i__2__n.

The jeweler's golden c__3__n was polished to a high l__4__r.

The i__5__e in the photo shows that both boys are of e__6__l height.

How would you i__7__e a math e__8__n?

The v__9__e weather kept Pat indoors in the r__10__n room.

The botanist wanted to c__11__e a new v__12__y of apples.

Use your c__13__y to draw an i__14__y animal.

Yumi was so i__15__e that she came up with v__16__s ways to solve the problem.

Juan's i__17__n is a v__18__n on a classic painting.

Can you i__19__e why the answers to his question may v__20__y?

For Tomorrow...
Be prepared to share your spelling words from book or movie reviews. Remember to study for the test!

Get Word Wise

In Latin, *lustrare* means "to light up." This meaning connects to *luster*, which means "shine." How would an *illustration* "light up"? Think of it this way. When you illustrate something with a picture, an act, or the words you speak, you light up an idea in the mind of the viewer or listener.

Word Study Strategy

See the word

Say it slowly

Link sounds and letters

Write

Check

END

LESSON
35

Spelling Words

occur
occurrence · LOOKOUT WORD
respect
respectful
disrespectful
disrespectfully
react
reaction
overreaction
sense
sensitive
sensitivity
insensitivity
grace
graceful
disgraceful
disgracefully
possible
impossible
impossibility

Review	Challenge
variable	establish
manufacture	antidisestablishmen-
disappointment	tarianism

My Words

_____

_____

_____

Word Building

A See and Say

The Spelling Concept

grace + -ful = graceful

dis- + graceful + -ly = disgracefully

Words built by adding prefixes and suffixes to the same base word are in the same family. Words built from the same base word are related in meaning and spelling.

The **r** in occurrence occurs more than once!

MEMORY JOGGER

B Link Sounds and Letters

Say each related group of spelling words. Listen for the same base word in each. Then sort all the spelling words into families on a diagram like the one below.

Word Sort

sense	grace	react	possible	respect	occur

C Write and Check

Rearrange the letters in *crate*. What spelling word do you get? _____

Rearrange the letters in *creation*. What spelling word do you get? _____

Now write a sentence, using one of these two new words.

_____

_____

A Build Vocabulary: Synonyms

Synonyms are words that have the same or almost the same meaning. Write the spelling word that is a synonym for each word.

1. respond
2. happen
3. aware
4. elegance
5. courteous
6. shamefully
7. happening
8. feel
9. unbelievable
10. admire
11. response
12. likely
13. awareness
14. elegant

B Prefixes and Suffixes

To solve the problems below, replace the definitions in quotes with the correct prefix or suffix. The chart tells what each one means. Put all the word parts together to form the spelling words.

dis-, im-, in-	=	not, opposite of
re-	=	again
over-	=	more than
-ful	=	filled with, full of
-ly	=	in a manner of

15. "not" + *respect* + "full of"
16. "not" + *respect* + "full of" + "in a manner of"
17. "more than" + "again" + *action*
18. "not" + *sensitivity*
19. "the opposite of" + *grace* + "filled with"
20. "not" + *possibility*

Be a Spelling Sleuth

Listen for your spelling words in news show discussions on TV or radio, and look for them in editorials in newspapers and magazines. Keep a list of each word you hear or read.

Spell Chat

With the person next to you, build some words by adding prefixes and suffixes. For example, if you say *grace*, your partner might say *graceful*, and then you might say *disgraceful*.

Spelling Words

occur	sensitive
occurrence LOOKOUT WORD	sensitivity
respect	insensitivity
respectful	grace
disrespectful	graceful
disrespectfully	disgraceful
react	disgracefully
reaction	possible
overreaction	impossible
sense	impossibility

Review	Challenge
variable	establish
manufacture	antidisestablishmen-
disappointment	tarianism

My Words

_____

_____

_____

Spelling Words

occur	sensitive
occurrence (LOOKOUT WORD)	sensitivity
respect	insensitivity
respectful	grace
disrespectful	graceful
disrespectfully	disgraceful
react	disgracefully
reaction	possible
overreaction	impossible
sense	impossibility

Review	Challenge
variable	establish
manufacture	antidisestablish-
disappointment	mentarianism

My Words

_____

_____

_____

Quick Write

Write two sentences that describe characters who might appear in a movie that you'd enjoy. Use at least one spelling word in each sentence.

A Write a Story Scene

You may wish to do this activity on a computer.

Imagine that you overhear two friends discussing a book they have both read. Write a story scene about this situation. Use dialogue to help reveal how the friends feel about the book. Be sure to use quotation marks.

B Proofread

Below is Marcel's scene about two friends discussing a book. He made five spelling errors, two quotation mark errors, one punctuation error, and one capitalization error. Correct them.

> **Tip**
>
> When you write, remember to enclose the exact words a speaker says in quotation marks.

"How did you react to the book," asked Carrie.

I thought it was written in a gracefull style, but I couldn't make sense of the plot," replied Leroy.

"Time travel seems like an imposibility, and dinosaurs roaming mars is an unlikely occurence. I simply did not find the book believable."

"I agree that the book was a dissappointment," said Leroy, but I think your opinion is an overeaction."

PROOFREADING MARKS

∧ Add

⅄ Add a comma

⅄⅄ Add quotation marks

⊙ Add a period

ℓ Take out

↶ Move

☰ Capital letter

/ Small letter

¢ Indent

Now proofread your story scene. Check your spelling, grammar, punctuation, and capitalization.

A Use the Dictionary: Accented Syllables

Look at the entry for *impossibility*. Notice the boldfaced syllable in the pronunciation. That syllable gets the strongest, or the primary, stress when you say the word. The syllable that appears in italic type gets the second greatest stress.

im•pos•si•bil•i•ty /im *pos* ə **bil** i tē/ *noun*
A condition that cannot be achieved, or something that cannot be true.

In your Spelling Dictionary, find three other words that have both primary and a secondary stress (Hint: many words with more than three syllables do). Say each word. Circle the syllables that get the primary stress and underline the syllables with the secondary stress.

_____

_____

_____

B Test Yourself

Use the code in the box below to decipher each spelling word.

sens = ▲	poss = ●	occu = ■
reac = ▼	resp = ★	grac = ✿

1. ▲e
2. ▼t
3. ★ectful
4. ✿e
5. dis✿efully
6. ■rrence
7. ★ect
8. ●ible
9. in▲itivity
10. over▼tion
11. dis★ectful
12. ▼tion
13. im●ibility
14. dis✿eful
15. ■r
16. im●ible
17. ▲itive
18. ✿eful
19. ▲itivity
20. dis★ectfully

For Tomorrow...
Be prepared to share the spelling words you heard on TV or radio. Remember to study for your test!

Get Word Wise

The word *grace* comes from the Latin word *gratus*, which means "pleasing." Other English words that contain the word part *grat* are *grateful*, *ingratiate*, and *gratification*. What do you think these words mean?

Word Study Strategy

See the word

Say it slowly

Link sounds and letters

Write

Check

END

Veterinarian in ACTION

Write words from the box to complete the paragraphs.

creativity **tempo** **disrespectful**
recreation **community**

A n animal clinic serves a useful role in a __(1)__ . As a veterinarian, I know that the __(2)__ at an animal clinic can be hectic. Animals are often very anxious patients, and it takes a lot of __(3)__ to keep them calm. Often I allow dogs to run off some of their excess energy in the dog run. One dog enjoyed the __(4)__ so much that I couldn't coax it out. Finally, I had to physically pick up the dog and carry it to the examination table. The dog made it clear that it was not happy by snarling and other __(5)__ behavior. After I gave it a treat, though, it settled down and let me examine it.

temporary **commonplace** **timeworn**
uncommon **imagination** **variable**

It may not be just the owner's __(6)__ when a pet seems to have caught a cold. In fact, a pet with a cold is not __(7)__ or unusual. In an animal clinic, such a sight is quite __(8)__ . The symptoms that a sick pet may have are __(9)__ , and not all pets show the same ones. An otherwise happy pet that acts dull and tired may have a __(10)__ illness. Most pet owners recognize the __(11)__ truth that sick animals do not behave normally.

occurrence **chaos** **characteristic**
choir **memorable**

Every day in the clinic, there is at least one noteworthy __(12)__ . One day, a basset hound began to howl. Before long, a whole __(13)__ of pets joined in the singing. This encouraged the basset hound, and it gave a particularly __(14)__ performance. The calm that was __(15)__ or typical of the clinic had been broken. Everything was in __(16)__ . What did I do? I took the basset hound and its owner into a separate room. Soon the other owners were able to quiet their pets, and peace was restored.

Find That Synonym

A synonym is a word that has the same, or nearly the same, meaning as another word. Find synonyms for each word below.

chaos   memento

possible

memorial   memoir

communication

1. souvenir _____

2. diary _____

3. probable _____

4. conversation _____

5. monument _____

6. confusion _____

All in the Family

Like people, words can be related. Teaming words in their word families can help you understand their meanings. Read each sentence, and write the Review Word that is related to each underlined word.

disgraceful disgracefully

disrespectful disrespectfully

imaginary imaginative

sensitivity insensitivity

reaction overreaction

TRY THIS

The Latin root *temp* means "time." Now take the time to write four words that use the English word *time* and four that use the Latin root *temp*.

_____

_____

_____

_____

_____

_____

_____

Imagine how wonderful it would be to spend a day at an athletic event.

7. _____   8. _____

You could sense the excitement as the crowd cheered for the home team.

9. _____   10. _____

The gymnastics team performed with grace and style.

11. _____   12. _____

I really respect the way they handle the stress of the competition.

13. _____   14. _____

How did Corina react when she received a 10 for her floor exercise?

15. _____   16. _____

untimely	impossibility
illustration	various
variation	interrupt
create	possible
temporarily	contemporary

Tip
Remember that you form possessive nouns with an 's.

Amazing Pet Tricks

Imagine you have a pet that does amazing tricks. You decide to make a video about it. You plan to submit your video to the producer of a TV program. You hope to make your pet a star! Describe what you will show in each scene of your video. Use a few Review Words in each scene description. Also, use your imagination and sense of humor.

Favorite Pet Tricks - Scene 1

_____

_____

_____

_____

_____

Favorite Pet Tricks - Scene 2

_____

_____

_____

_____

_____

Look back at the words you misspelled in your Unit 6 Posttests. Use them to write an additional scene description.

Tell About It

Choose one of your scene descriptions, and write a journal entry about how you taught your pet the trick in question. Proofread your work for spelling, capitalization, grammar, and punctuation.

PROOFREADING MARKS

∧   Add
⋏   Add a comma
⌄⌄   Add quotation marks
⊙   Add a period
ℓ   Take out
◯⌆   Move
≡   Capital letter
／   Small letter
¢   Indent

Write It Right!

As the editor of the school newspaper, you are putting the finishing touches on the articles for this week's issue. You want to make sure you spell all the words correctly. Use each set of words below to complete the articles.

chameleon   mechanical   chemistry

1. Last week the biology class lost its pet _____. The class looked everywhere for the missing pet and finally

found it in the _____ lab. A relieved student said

that she was glad the pet had not caused a _____ problem by crawling into the heating system.

architect   chronicle

2. For American history, fifth graders have read *The Civil War: A True Story*. It explodes with real-life adventure. A young boy

becomes the brilliant _____ of a plan that helps President Lincoln. The story is based on facts from a recently

discovered daily _____ from the era.

character   archive

3. The library now has an _____ of photos showing students who have attended this school since its founding in 1920. Don't be surprised if you see pictures of a

_____ or two that you find amusing.

architecture   chronological

4. With our new video collection, you can explore buildings, old

and new. Take a _____ survey, beginning with the pyramids of ancient Egypt and ending with present-

day skyscrapers. Enjoy the _____ of buildings, ranging from the past to the present.

Nina says...

In advertising we use words and pictures to convey messages. Once we were preparing a food ad for a client. The ad said, "Magna's new microwave oven is a real timeshaver." If the copy editor had not found the error, we would have been embarrassed. Of course, the ad should have said, "Magna's new microwave oven is a real timesaver." That oven doesn't shave time, it saves it!

Spelling Matters!

A B C D E F G
H I J K L M N
O P Q R S T U
V W X Y Z

a b c d e f g h i j
k l m n o p q r s t
u v w x y z

Commonly Misspelled Words

advice	communication	formula	physician	solemn
advise	competition	illustration	poetic	species
a lot	compromise	imagination	possible	substitute
analyze	condemn	impossibility	potatoes	subterranean
appreciate	creativity	improvise	precede	syllable
appreciation	criticize	instinct	proceed	sympathy
artificial	cylinder	interrupt	receipt	syrup
association	deceitful	manufacturer	receiver	system
athlete	definition	mechanical	relieve	televise
autumn	desert	memoir	remembrance	temporarily
beneficial	dessert	missile	rhyme	temporary
benefit	disaster	moral	rhythm	terrarium
cereal	disguise	morale	sense	theater
characteristic	dismissal	multiplication	sensitive	theatrical
chiefs	educator	no one	series	unique
chord	evidence	occurrence	sheriffs	universal
chorus	exhibit	o'clock	similar	utilize
civilization	explanation	overwhelmed	skiing	variety
committee	extension	oxygen	soccer	visible
communicate	fascinate	physical	society	wherever

All your spelling words appear in alphabetical order in this Spelling Dictionary. The labeled entry on this page shows you how to use the Spelling Dictionary to find useful information about the words.

The **entry word** is the word you look up. This shows you how the word is divided into syllables.

This shows you the **pronunciation** of the entry word.

These are the **definitions** of the entry word. This word has two different meanings.

This tells you the **part of speech** of the entry word. Sometimes an entry word can be used as two or more different parts of speech.

coun·sel /koun səl/
1. *verb* To listen to people's problems and give advice. **2.** *noun* Advice.
    Counsel sounds like **council**.
▶ *verb* **counseling, counseled**

These are other **forms** of the entry word. You might use them to check your spelling when you use the words in writing.

Other information comes after the definitions of some entry words. Here you might find the Greek or Latin root of the entry word, or your Spelling Dictionary may mention another word that sounds the same.

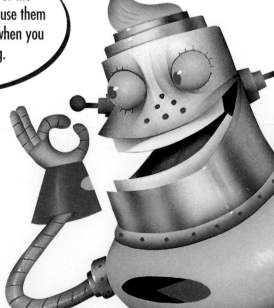

A a

a·chieve /ə chēv/ *verb*
To do something sucessfully, especially after a lot of effort.

a·dapt /ə dapt/ *verb*
To make suitable for a different purpose.

ad·mis·sion /ad mish ən/ *noun*
1. Right of entry; entrance fee.
2. A confession.

ad·mit /ad mit/ *verb*
1. To confess to doing, or agree that something is true, often reluctantly.
2. To allow to enter.
from Latin: ad- to + *mittere* to send

ad·mit·tance /ad mit ns/ *noun*
1. Permission or right to enter.
2. Actual entrance.

ad·mit·ting /ad mit ing/ *verb*
1. Confessing to something, or agreeing that something is true.
2. Allowing someone or something to enter.

a·dopt /ə dopt/ *verb*
1. To take a child into one's family and become his or her legal parents.
2. To accept an idea or a way of doing things.

ad·ver·tise /ad vər tīz/ *verb*
To give information about something you want to sell. ▶ **advertising, advertised** ▶ *noun* **advertiser**

ad·vice /ad vīs/ *noun*
A suggestion about what someone should do.

ad·vise /ad vīz/ *verb*
To give someone information or suggestions. ▶ **advising, advised**

air con·di·tion·er /âr kən dish ə nər/ *noun*
A machine that controls the temperature and humidity in a room or vehicle.

a lot /ə lot/ *adverb*
To a great degree; much.

al·pha·bet·ize /al fə bi tīz/ *verb*
To arrange a series of things so that they follow the order of the letters of the alphabet, from A to Z.

an·a·lyze /an l īz/ *verb*
To examine carefully.

an·chor /ang kər/
1. *noun* A heavy metal hook that is lowered from a ship or boat to keep it in place in water.
2. *verb* To hold firmly in place.

an·ti·dis·es·tab·lish·men·tar·i·an·ism
/an tē dis ə stab lish mən târ ē ə niz əm/ *noun*
Opposition to the idea that church and state should be separate.

an·to·nym /an tə nim/ *noun*
A word that means the opposite of another word.

a·piece /ə pēs/ *adverb*
Each, or each one.

a·pol·o·gize /ə pol ə jīz/ *verb*
To say that you are sorry about something.

ap·pre·ci·ate /ə prē shē āt/ *verb*
1. To enjoy and understand. 2. To be thankful for something. 3. To increase in worth.

ap·pre·ci·a·tion
/ə prē shē ā shən/ *noun*
1. Enjoyment and understanding.
2. A feeling or expression of
thankfulness. 3. A rise in price or
value.

aq·ue·duct /ak wi *dukt*/ *noun*
A large bridge built to carry water
across a valley or over a river; a
channel that carries water from a
distant source.
from Latin: aqua water + *ducere* to
lead

ar·chi·tect /är ki *tekt*/ *noun*
A person who designs buildings.

ar·chi·tec·ture
/är ki *tek* chər/ *noun*
1. The art of designing buildings.
2. The style of a building.

ar·chive /är kīv/
1. *noun* A place where public
records or historical documents
are preserved. 2. *verb* To file or
collect records or documents in,
or as if in, an archive.

ar·ti·fact /är tə *fakt*/ *noun*
An object made or changed by
human beings; especially a tool or
weapon used in the past.
from Latin: ars- art + *facere* to
make

ar·ti·fi·cial /är tə *fish* əl/
adjective False, not real or natural.
from Latin: ars- art + *facere* to
make

as·so·ci·ate
1. /ə sō shē āt/ *verb* To connect in
one's mind: *I associate pumpkins
with Halloween.* 2. /ə sō shē āt/
verb To join as a partner, member,
or friend. 3. /ə sō shē it/ *noun* A
partner or friend.
from Latin: sociare to join

as·so·ci·a·tion
/ə sō sē ā shən/ *noun*
1. An organization, club, or
society. 2. A connection that you
make in your mind between
thoughts and feelings and a
person or thing.

as·ter /as tər/ *noun*
A plant related to the daisy, with
star-shaped flowers.
from Greek: aster star

as·ter·isk /as tə risk/ *noun*
The symbol (*) used in printing
and writing to tell readers to look
elsewhere on the page for more
information.

Word History

Asterisk comes from the Greek
word *asteriskos*, which means
"little star."

as·ter·oid /as tə roid/ *noun*
A very small planetlike mass that
orbits around the sun.
from Greek: aster star

as·tro·dome /as trə dōm/
noun A transparent dome for
housing astronomical or
navigational instruments,
especially in an airplane.
from Greek: astro star

as·tro·naut /as trə nôt/ *noun*
A person who travels in space.
from Greek: astro star + *naut* sailor

as·tron·o·mer /ə stron ə
mər/ *noun*
A person who studies astronomy.
from Greek: astro star

as·tro·nom·i·cal
/as trə nom i kəl/ *adjective*
1. To do with astronomy. *The
planetarium shows astronomical
films.* 2. Very large, as in *an
astronomical amount of money.*
from Greek: astro star

as·tron·o·my /ə stron ə mē/
noun The study of stars, planets,
and space.
from Greek: astro star + *nomos*
system of laws

as·tro·phys·ics
/as trō fiz iks/ *noun*
A branch of astronomy dealing
with the physical properties and
processes of stars and planets.
from Greek: astro star

a·sym·met·ri·cal
/ā sə me trik əl/ *adjective*
A shape that cannot be divided so that both pieces match exactly in size and shape.

ath·lete /ath lēt/ *noun*
Someone who is trained in or very good at sports or games that require strength, speed, and/or skill.

ath·let·ic /ath let ik/ *adjective*
Physically active, strong, and good at sports.

au·di·ble /ô də bəl/ *adjective*
Loud enough to be heard.
from Latin: audire to hear

au·di·ence /ô dē əns/ *noun*
A group of people who watch or listen to a performance, speech, or movie.
from Latin: audire to hear

au·di·o /ô dē ō/ *adjective*
Of or relating to sound or hearing.
from Latin: audire to hear

au·di·o·vis·u·al
/ô dē ō vizh ōō əl/ *adjective*
Of or relating to equipment that uses sound and pictures, often for teaching purposes.
from Latin: audire to hear + visus sight

au·di·tion /ô dish ən/ *noun*
A short performance by a performer to see whether he or she is suitable for a part in a play, concert, etc.
from Latin: audire to hear

au·di·to·ri·um
/ô di tôr ē əm/ *noun*
A building or large room where people gather for meetings, plays, concerts, or other events.
from Latin: audire to hear

au·thor·i·za·tion
/ô thər ə zā shən/ *noun*
Official permission. *The principal gave us authorization to hold a fund-raiser.*

au·thor·ize /ô thə rīz/ *verb*
To give official permission for something to happen.
▶ **authorizing, authorized**

au·tumn /ô təm/ *noun*
The season between summer and winter; fall.

B b

bank·rupt /bangk rupt/
adjective Unable to pay one's debts.
from Latin: banca bank + rumpere to break

bank·rupt·cy
/bangk rupt sē/ *noun*
The state of being bankrupt.
from Latin: banca bank + rumpere to break

bar·be·cue /bär bi kyōō/
1. *noun* A charcoal grill used for cooking meat and other food outdoors. 2. *noun* A meal, usually outdoors, in which food is cooked in this manner. 3. *verb* To broil or roast over an open fire.

bar·ri·cade /bar i kād/
1. *noun* A barrier to stop people from getting past a certain point.
2. *verb* To build walls or other obstacles to stop people from reaching someone or something.

base·ball /bās bôl/ *noun*
1. A game played with a bat and ball and two teams of nine players each. 2. The ball used in this game.

bas·ket·ball /bas kit bôl/ *noun*
1. A game played by two teams of five players each that try to score points by throwing a ball through a high net at the end of a court. 2. The large, round ball used in this game.

ben·e·fi·cial /ben ə fish əl/
adjective Helpful; good for. *Eating vegetables is beneficial to your health.*
from Latin: bene good, well + facere to make

a	add	ô	order	ŧh	this
ā	ace	ōō	took	zh	vision
â	care	ōō	pool		
ä	palm	u	up		
e	end	û	burn	ə	=
ē	equal	yōō	fuse	a	in *above*
i	it	oi	oil	e	in *sicken*
ī	ice	ou	pout	i	in *possible*
o	odd	ng	ring	o	in *melon*
ō	open	th	thin	u	in *circus*

ben·e·fit /ben ə fit/ *verb*
To receive help or receive an advantage from.
*from Latin: bene good, well +
facere to do or make*

brief /brēf/
1. *adjective* Lasting only a short time. 2. *adjective* Using only a few words. 3. *verb* To give someone information so that the person can carry out a task. 4. *noun* An outline of the main information and arguments of a legal case.
▶ *adjective* briefer, briefest
▶ *adverb* briefly

brothers·in·law
/bruŧħ ərs in lô/ *noun*
The brothers of one's husband or wife, or the husbands of one's sisters.

brunch (breakfast + lunch)
/brunch/ *noun*
A meal usually eaten in the late morning that combines a late breakfast and an early lunch.

buf·fet
1. /buf it/ *verb* To strike or shake someone or something. 2. /bə fā/ *noun* A meal in which many foods are laid out on a table and people serve themselves.

C c

calves /kavz/ *noun*
1. Young cows, seals, elephants, giraffes, or whales. 2. The fleshy part at the back of your legs, below the knee. *singular* calf

cap·size /kap sīz/ *verb*
To turn over in the water.
▶ capsizing, capsized

care·free /kâr frē/ *adjective*
Being without anxiety or worry.

cat·e·go·rize /kat i gə rīz/
verb To classify; to divide or group according to a system.

cen·ten·ni·al /sen ten ē əl/
noun The celebration of a hundredth anniversary.
from Latin: centum hundred

cen·ti·grade /sen ti grād/
adjective A measurement of temperature using a scale on which water boils at 100 degrees and freezes at 0 degrees. It is also called **Celsius**.
*from Latin: centum hundred +
gradus degree*

cen·ti·me·ter /sen tə mē tər/
noun A unit of length in the metric system, equal to 1/100 of a meter.
*from Latin: centum hundred +
metrum measure*

cen·ti·pede /sen tə pēd/
noun A wormlike animal with many pairs of legs.
*from Latin: centum hundred + pes
foot*

cen·tu·ry /sen chə rē/ *noun*
A period of 100 years.
from Latin: centum hundred

ce·re·al /sēr ē əl/ *noun*
1. A grain crop grown for food, such as wheat, corn, oats, rice, or barley. 2. A breakfast food usually made from grain and eaten with milk. **Cereal** sounds like **serial**.

cha·me·le·on /kə mē lē ən/
noun A lizard that can change color, sometimes matching its surroundings.

cha·os /kā os/ *noun*
A state of total confusion.

cha·o·tic /kā ot ik/ *adjective*
In a state of confusion and disorder.

char·ac·ter /kar ik tər/ *noun*
1. The qualities and features that identify a person or thing. 2. One of the people in a story, book, play, movie, or television program.

char·ac·ter·is·tic
/kar ik tə ris tik/
1. *noun* A typical quality or feature. 2. *adjective* Typical.

char·ac·ter·ize
/kar ik te rīz/ *verb*
1. To describe the individual qualities of something or someone. 2. To identify the important qualities of something or someone.

cheer·lead·er /chēr lē dər/
noun A person who leads spectators in organized cheering, especially at an athletic event.

chem·i·cal /kem i kəl/
1. *noun* A substance used in chemistry. 2. *adjective* To do with or made by chemistry, as in a *chemical reaction*.

chem·ist /kem ist/ *noun*
A person trained in chemistry.

che·mis·try /kem ə strē/
noun The scientific study of substances, what they are composed of, and the ways in which they react with one another.

chiefs /chēfs/ *noun*
The leaders of groups of people.

choir /kwīr/ *noun*
A group of people who sing together.

cho·les·ter·ol /kə les tə rōl/
noun A fatty substance that humans and animals need to digest food and produce certain vitamins and hormones.

cho·ral /kôr əl/ *adjective*
Sung by a choir, as in *choral music*.

chord /kôrd/ *noun*
1. A combination of musical notes played at the same time. 2. A straight line that joins two points on a curve.

cho·re·og·ra·phy
/kôr ē og rə fē/ *noun*
The art of arranging dance steps and movements for a ballet or show.

cho·rus /kôr əs/ *noun*
1. The part of a song that is repeated after each verse. 2. A large group of people who sing or speak together. *plural* **choruses**

chron·ic /kron ik/ *adjective*
Lasting for a long period of time.
from Greek: chronos time

chron·i·cle /kron i kəl/
1. *verb* To record historical events in a careful, detailed way, usually in the order they happened.
2. *noun* Such a record.
from Greek: chronos time

chron·o·log·i·cal
/kron l oj i kəl/ *adjective*
Arranged in the order in which events happened.
from Greek: chronos time + *logos* speech

civ·i·li·za·tion
/siv ə lə zā shən/ *noun*
1. An advanced stage of human society, organization, technology, and culture.
2. A highly developed and organized society, as in *the ancient civilizations of Greece and Rome*.

civ·i·lize /siv ə līz/ *verb*
1. To improve someone's manners and education. 2. To improve a society so that it is better organized and its people have a higher standard of living.
from Latin: civis citizen
▶ **civilizing, civilized**

com·mit /kə mit/ *verb*
1. To do; perform. 2. To promise to do a certain course of activity.
from Latin: com- with + *mittere* to send

com·mit·ment /kə mit mənt/
noun 1. A promise. 2. The act of commiting.

com·mit·tee /kə mit ē/ *noun*
A group of people chosen to discuss things and make decisions for a larger group.

com·mon /kom ən/ *adjective*
1. Existing in large numbers.
2. Happening often. 3. Ordinary; not special. 4. Shared by two or more people or things.
from Latin: communis common

com·mon·ly /kom ən lē/
adverb Usually; frequently.

com·mon·place
/kom ən plās/ *adjective*
Ordinary; not new.

a	add	ô	order	ŧħ	this
ā	ace	ōō	took	zh	vision
â	care	ōō	pool		
ä	palm	u	up		
e	end	û	burn	ə	=
ē	equal	yōō	fuse	a	in *above*
i	it	oi	oil	e	in *sicken*
ī	ice	ou	pout	i	in *possible*
o	odd	ng	ring	o	in *melon*
ō	open	th	thin	u	in *circus*

com·mu·ni·cate
/kə myōō ni kāt/ *verb*
To share information, ideas, or feelings with another person by talking, writing, and so on.
from Latin: communis common
▶ communicating, communicated

com·mu·ni·ca·tion
/kə myōō ni kā shən/ *noun*
1. The act of sharing information.
2. Information or ideas that are communicated.

com·mu·ni·ty
/kə myōō ni tē/ *noun*
A group of people who live in the same area or who have something in common with one another.
from Latin: communis common
plural communities

com·pare /kəm pâr/ *verb*
To judge one thing against another and notice similarities and differences.

com·par·i·son
/kəm par ə sən/ *noun*
The act of comparing; the state of being compared.

com·pete /kəm pēt/ *verb*
To try hard to outdo others at a task, race, or contest.
▶ competing, competed

com·pe·ti·tion
/kom pi tish ən/ *noun*
A situation in which two or more people are trying to get the same thing.

com·ple·ment
/kom plə mənt/
1. *noun* Something that completes something or makes a thing whole and perfect. *The new stamp is the perfect complement to my current collection.* 2. *verb* To make whole or complete.
Complement sounds like **compliment**.

com·pli·ment
/kom plə mənt/
1. *verb* To tell a person that you admire him or her; to give praise.
2. *noun* An expression of praise.
Compliment sounds like **complement**.

com·pose /kəm pōz/ *verb*
1. To write or create music, poetry or art. *Mozart composed symphonies.* 2. To make up something. *Water is composed of hydrogen and oxygen.*

com·po·si·tion
/kom pə zish ən/ *noun*
1. The combining of parts to form a whole. 2. What something is made of. 3. Something that is created; especially a written work.

com·pro·mise
/kom prə mīz/
1. *verb* To agree to accept something that is not exactly what you wanted. 2. *noun* An agreement reached after people with opposing views each give up some of their demands.

con·ceit·ed /kən sē tid/
adjective Having a very favorable opinion of oneself.

con·demn /kən dem/ *verb*
1. To express strong disapproval of someone or something. 2. To punish. *The robber was condemned to twenty years in prison.* 3. To state that something is unsafe and should not be used.

con·duct
1. /kən dukt/ *verb* To lead or carry out. 2. /kən dukt/ *verb* To direct musicians. 3. /kən dukt/ *verb* To allow heat, electricity, or other energy to pass through.
4. /kon dukt/ *noun* Behavior. *Mauricio was awarded a prize for good conduct.*
from Latin: conducere to lead

con·duc·ting /kən duk ting/
verb 1. Leading or guiding.
2. Serving as a channel or medium for heat, electricity, or sound.

con·duc·tor /kən duk tər/
noun 1. A person who guides or leads. 2. Someone who collects railroad or bus fares.
3. A substance that allows heat, electricity, or sound to travel through it.

con·form /kən fôrm/ *verb*
1. To behave in the same way as everyone else or in a way that is expected of you. 2. To follow a set standard or rule. *All restaurants must conform to health codes.*

con·form·ing /kən fôr ming/
verb 1. Behaving in the same way as everyone else or in a way that is expected of you. **2.** Following a set standard or rule.

con·ser·va·tion
/kon sər vā shən/ **noun**
The protection of valuable things, especially wildlife and natural resources.

con·serve /kən sûrv/ **verb**
To save something from loss, decay, or waste; to preserve. *We turn out the lights when we leave the room in order to conserve energy.*

con·stel·la·tion
/kon stə lā shən/ **noun**
A group of stars that forms a shape or pattern.

con·tem·po·rar·y
/kən tem pə rer ē/ **adjective**
1. Up-to-date; modern. **2.** Living or occurring during the same period of time.
from Latin: tempus time

cor·rupt /kə rupt/
1. adjective Having poor morals; dishonest. **2. verb** To make someone bad or dishonest.

could·n't /kŏŏd nt/ **contraction**
A short form of **could not**. *Jesse couldn't write his report until he did some research.*

coun·cil /koun səl/ **noun**
A group of people chosen to look after the interests of a town, a county, or an organization, as in *the city council*.
Council sounds like **counsel**.

coun·sel /koun səl/
1. verb To listen to people's problems and give advice.
2. noun Advice.
▶ **verb counseling, counseled**
Counsel sounds like **council**.

court·house /kôrt hous/ **noun**
A building where trials and government business are conducted.

cre·ate /krē āt/ **verb**
To make or design something.

cre·a·tion /krē ā shən/ **noun**
1. Something that has been made.
2. The act of making something.

cre·a·tive /krē ā tiv/ **adjective**
Able to create things; good at thinking of new ideas and using your imagination.

cre·a·tiv·i·ty /krē ā tiv i tē/
noun The quality of being creative.

crit·i·cize /krit ə sīz/ **verb**
1. To find fault with someone or something. **2.** To point out the good and bad parts of a book, movie, play, etc. ▶ **criticizing, criticized**

cyl·in·der /sil in dər/ **noun**
A solid or hollow round shape with circular ends. *A tube is a cylinder.*

cym·bal /sim bəl/ **noun**
A musical instrument made of brass and shaped like a plate. **Cymbal** sounds like **symbol**.

D d

da·ta /dā tə/ **noun** Information.

day·time /dā tīm/ **noun**
The hours of daylight from dawn till dusk.

dead end /ded end/
1. noun A street that is closed to traffic at one end. **2. dead-end adjective** Leading nowhere. *Pete is worried that he has a dead-end job.*

dec·ade /dek ād/ **noun**
A period of ten years.
from Greek: deca ten

de·cath·lon /di kath lon/
noun A track-and-field contest made up of ten athletic events.
from Greek: deca ten + athlos contest

de·ceit·ful /di sēt fəl/ **adjective**
Given to lying or misleading others.

dec·i·mal /des ə məl/
1. adjective A system of counting and computation that has ten as its base. **2. noun** A fraction, or a whole number and a fraction, written with a decimal point.

a	add	ô	order	ͭħ	this
ā	ace	͞oͦ	took	zh	vision
â	care	͞oͦ	pool		
ä	palm	u	up		
e	end	û	burn	ə	=
ē	equal	yͦoͦ	fuse	a	in *above*
i	it	oi	oil	e	in *sicken*
ī	ice	ou	pout	i	in *possible*
o	odd	ng	ring	o	in *melon*
ō	open	th	thin	u	in *circus*

de·duc·tion /di duk shən/
noun **1.** An amount that is taken away or subtracted from a larger amount. **2.** Something that is figured out from clues.
from Latin: de- away + ducere to lead

def·ine /di fīn/ *verb*
To explain or describe something exactly. ▶ **defining, defined**

def·i·ni·tion /def ə nish ən/
noun An explanation of the meaning of a word or phrase.

de·moc·ra·cy /di mok rə sē/
noun **1.** A way of governing a country in which the people choose their leaders in elections. **2.** A country that has an elected government. *The United States is a democracy.* **plural democracies**

dem·o·crat·ic /dem ə krat ik/
adjective **1.** To do with or in favor of democracy. **2.** Relating to a system in which all people have equal rights.

dem·on·stra·tion
/dem ən strā shən/ *noun*
1. The act of proving something. *Her rescue of the drowning boy was a demonstration of bravery.* **2.** Explaining or showing a process through description, experiment or example. *The teacher held a demonstration to show how electricity is conducted.* **3.** A public gathering to show feeling toward a particular issue or person. *The people held a demonstration to help save the park.*

des·ert
1. /di zûrt/ *verb* To abandon someone or something, or to run away from the army. *The captain deserted his troops.* **2.** /dez ərt/ *noun* A dry, often sandy area where few plants grow because there is so little rain.

de·spise /di spīz/ *verb*
To dislike greatly.

des·sert /di zûrt/ *noun*
A food, such as ice cream, fruit, or cake, usually served at the end of a meal.

die·sel /dē zəl/
1. *noun* A fuel that is heavier than gasoline. **2.** *adjective* Describing a machine or vehicle powered by an engine that burns fuel oil using heat produced by compressing air. [named after Rudolf Diesel, (1858–1913), a German engineer and the engine's inventor.]

di·gest
1. /di jest/ *verb* To break down food so that it can be absorbed into the blood and used by the body. **2.** To think something over for a time to gain a better understanding. *It is difficult to digest a lot of information at once.* **3.** /dī jest/ *noun* A shortened form of a book or other written work, or a collection of such shortened forms.

di·ges·tion /di jes chən/ *noun*
The process of breaking down food in the stomach and other organs so that it can be absorbed into the body.

dis·as·ter /di zas tər/ *noun*
1. An event that creates great damage or loss, such as a flood. **2.** Something that turns out completely wrong.

dis·as·trous /di zas trəs/
adjective Causing great distress or injury.

dis·grace·ful /dis grās fəl/
adjective Causing or deserving shame or disapproval.

dis·grace·ful·ly
/dis grās fəl ē/ *adverb*
With disgrace; shamefully.

dis·guise /dis gīz/
1. *verb* To hide something. **2.** *noun* Something worn to hide your identity.
▶ *verb* disguising, disguised

dis·in·ter·est·ed
/dis in tə res tid/ *adjective*
Impartial, or without personal feelings for either side of a contest or an argument.

dis·lo·cate
/dis lō kāt/ or /dis lō kāt/ *verb*
1. To put out of place. **2.** To put out of joint or position, as a shoulder. **3.** To upset or throw out of order. ▶ **dislocating, dislocated**

dis·miss /dis mis/ *verb*
1. To direct or allow to leave. **2.** To fire someone from a job. **3.** To put something out of your mind.

dis·mis·sal /dis mis əl/ *noun*
The act of dismissing; the fact or state of being dismissed.

dis·re·spect·ful
/dis ri **spekt** fəl/ *adjective*
Having or showing a lack of respect; rude.

dis·re·spect·ful·ly
/dis ri **spekt** fəl lē/ *adverb*
In a way that shows a lack of respect.

dis·rupt /dis **rupt**/ *verb*
To disturb or break up.
from Latin: dis- apart + *rumpere* to break

dis·sat·is·fac·tion
/dis sat is **fak** shən/ *noun*
The state or attitude of not being satisfied; disappointment.

di·vide /di **vīd**/ *verb*
1. To split into parts. 2. In math, to determine how many times one number will go into another. 3. To share.

di·vi·sion /di **vizh** ən/ *noun*
1. In mathematics, the act of dividing one number by another.
2. One of the sections or parts into which something larger has been divided. 3. Something that separates. 4. A military unit.

dom·i·noes /**dom** ə nōs/ *noun*
1. Small, rectangular tiles that are divided into two halves that are blank or have dots. 2. A game played with a number of these tiles.

do·nate /**dō** nāt/ *verb*
To give as a present; contribute.
▶ **donating, donated**

do·na·tion /dō **nā** shən/ *noun*
1. The act of donating.
2. Something donated; a contribution or gift.

dou·ble·head·er
/**dub** əl hed ər/ *noun*
Two baseball games played one right after another.

dram·a·tize /**dram** ə tīz/ *verb*
1. To adapt a story into a play.
2. To express in a vivid or intense and sometimes exaggerated way.
▶ **dramatizing, dramatized**

drive-in /**drīv** in/ *adjective*
Designed so that customers may be served or entertained in their cars. *Between 1947 and 1950 over 2,000 drive-in movie theaters opened in the United States.*

duct /**dukt**/ *noun*
A tube that carries air or liquid from one place to another.
from Latin: ducere to lead

du·pli·cate
1. /**doo** pli kāt/ *verb* To make an exact copy of something.
2. /**doo** pli kit/ *noun* An exact copy. 3. /**doo** pli kit/ *adjective* Exactly like or corresponding to something else. *verb* **duplicating, duplicated**

du·pli·ca·tion
/**doo** pli kā shən/ *noun*
1. The act or process of copying.
2. A copy.

E e

earth·bound /**ûrth** bound/
adjective 1. Located on or limited to the surface of the earth.
2. Lacking in imagination.

earth·ling /**ûrth** ling/ *noun*
A person or creature who lives on the earth.

earth·ly /**ûrth** lē/ *adjective*
1. Characteristic of or belonging to the earth. 2. Possible to imagine.

earth·mov·er /**ûrth** moo vər/
noun A machine, such as a bulldozer, for digging, pushing, or moving large amounts of earth.

earth·quake /**ûrth** kwāk/
noun A sudden, violent shaking of the earth, caused by a shifting of the earth's crust.

earth·shak·ing
/**ûrth** shā king/ *adjective*
Of great importance.
Synonym: momentous

earth·worm /**ûrth** wûrm/ *noun*
A gray, pink, red, or brown worm that digs through the ground and eats the nutrients in dirt.

a	add	ô	order	<u>th</u>	this
ā	ace	oo	took	zh	vision
â	care	oo	pool		
ä	palm	u	up		
e	end	û	burn	ə	=
ē	equal	yoo	fuse	a	in *above*
i	it	oi	oil	e	in *sicken*
ī	ice	ou	pout	i	in *possible*
o	odd	ng	ring	o	in *melon*
ō	open	th	thin	u	in *circus*

eas·el /ē zəl/ *noun* A folding stand used to support a painting, sign, and so on.

ech·oes /ek ōz/
1. *noun* Repeated sounds produced by the reflection of sound waves off a wall, mountain, or other surface. **2.** *verb* To send back the sound of something. *The mountain echoes our cries.*
singular echo

ed·u·cate /ej ōō kāt/ *verb* To give knowledge or a skill; teach.
from Latin: ducere to lead

ed·u·ca·tion /ej ōō kā shən/ *noun* **1.** The process of educating. **2.** The knowledge, skills, and abilities gained from schooling.

ed·u·ca·tor /ej ōō kā tər/ *noun* A person who educates; a teacher.

ef·fect /i fekt/ *noun*
1. *noun* The result or consequence of something. *One effect of the storm was a citywide blackout.*
2. *noun* Influence, or the power to make something happen. *The President's speech had a great effect on him.* **3.** *noun* The state of being in operation. **4.** *verb* To cause to happen.
from Latin: facere to do

ef·fec·tive /i fek tiv/ *adjective*
1. Working very well, or getting the job done. **2.** In force. *The new rule will become effective next year.*

eigh·ty /ā tē/ *noun*
The number that is eight times ten.

em·i·gra·tion /em i grā shən/ *noun* The process or act of leaving your own country to live in another one.

em·pha·size /em fə sīz/ *verb* To make something important stand out clearly; to stress.
▶ **emphasizing, emphasized**

en·e·mies' /en ə mēs/ *noun, possessive of* enemies
1. Of or belonging to a group of people who hate, oppose, or want to harm or destroy another group or person. **2.** Of or belonging to countries or armies that you are fighting against in a war.

en·e·my's /en ə mēs/ *noun, possessive of* enemy
1. Of or belonging to someone who hates and wants to harm or destroy another. **2.** Of or belonging to the country or army that you are fighting against in a war.

e·qual /ē kwəl/
1. *adjective* The same as something else in size, value or amount. *Two pints are equal to one quart.*
2. *adjective* The same for each member of a group, as in *equal housing opportunities.* **3.** *noun* A person of equal ability or position, or a thing of equal quality, as in *a jury of one's equals.* **4.** *verb* To be or become equal to; to match. *John will equal Carla's skills on the ball field.*

e·qua·tion /i kwā zhən/ *noun* A mathematical statement that one set of numbers or values is equal to another set of numbers or values. For example, *4 x 4 = 16.*

e·rode /i rōd/ *verb* To gradually wear away, especially by water or wind.

e·ro·sion /i rō zhən/ *noun* The gradual wearing away of a substance by water or wind, as in *beach erosion.*

es·tab·lish /i stab lish/ *verb*
1. To begin or set up, as in a business. **2.** To settle somewhere. **3.** To confirm that something is true or correct.

eve·ry·bod·y /ev rē bod ē/ *pronoun* Each and every person.

eve·ry·thing /ev rē thing/ *pronoun* **1.** Each and every thing. **2.** A very important thing. *Our friendship means everything to me.*

ev·i·dence /ev i dəns/ *noun* Information and facts that help prove something or make you believe that something is true.

ev·i·dent /ev i dənt/ *adjective* Clear and obvious.

ex·claim /ik sklām/ *verb* To say something suddenly or with force, especially because you are surprised or excited.

ex·cla·ma·tion /ek sklə mā shən/ *noun* A sharp or sudden outcry; a word or phrase spoken loudly or with vigor.

ex·clude /ik sklo͞od/ *verb*
1. To leave out or omit. 2. To keep out or prevent someone from joining. ▶ **excluding, excluded**

ex·clu·sion /ik sklo͞o zhən/ *noun* 1. An act or instance of excluding. 2. The state of being left out or excluded.

ex·hale /eks hāl/ *verb* To breathe out. ▶ **exhaling, exhaled**

ex·hib·it /ig zib it/
1. *verb* To show or demonstrate. *In her essay she exhibits a deep understanding of the poem.* 2. *verb* To present to the public. 3. *noun* A display, as at a museum or gallery.

ex·plain /ik splān/ *verb*
1. To make something clear so that it is easier to understand. 2. To give a reason for something.

ex·pla·na·tion /ek splə nā shən/ *noun*
1. The act or process of explaining. 2. Something that explains.

ex·por·ta·tion /ek spôr tā shən/ *noun*
The act of sending products to another country to be sold there.

ex·press /ik spres/
1. *verb* To show what you feel or think by saying, doing, or writing something. 2. *noun* A fast train or bus that stops only at a few stations. 3. *adjective* Very fast, as in *express delivery.*

ex·pres·sion /ik spresh ən/
noun 1. A phrase that has a particular meaning; a saying, as in *eat like a horse.* 2. The look on someone's face, as in *a puzzled expression.* 3. The act of showing your feelings.

ex·tend /ik stend/ *verb*
1. To make something longer or bigger. 2. To stretch out; reach. 3. To offer, as in *to extend help to flood victims.*
from Latin: ex- out + *tendere* to stretch

ex·ten·sion
/ik sten shən/
noun 1. The act of extending or condition of being extended.
2. An addition. *Our school built an extension to house the extra students.*
3. An increase in length of time.

ex·te·ri·or /ik stēr ē ər/ *noun*
The outside of something, especially a building.

ex·ter·nal /ik stûr nl/ *adjective*
On the outside.

ex·tinct /ik stingkt/ *adjective*
1. No longer existing, due to dying out, as in *extinct animal* or *extinct plant.* 2. Inactive, as in *extinct volcano.*

F f

fac·sim·i·le /fak sim ə lē/
noun 1. An exact copy. 2. An exact copy sent by a special machine over telephone lines.

fact /fakt/ *noun*
A piece of information that is true.

fac·tor /fak tər/ *noun*
1. Something that helps produce a result. *Randy's new training schedule was a factor in his winning the race.* 2. A whole number that can be divided exactly into a larger number. *The numbers 1, 2, 3, 4, 6, and 12 are factors of 12.*

fac·to·ry /fak tə rē/ *noun*
A building where products such as cars or chemicals are made in large numbers, often using machines.
from Latin: facere to do
plural factories

fac·tu·al /fak cho͞o əl/ *adjective*
Based on facts. *The news story gave a factual account of the meeting.*

fas·ci·nate /fas ə nāt/ *verb*
To attract and hold the attention of. ▶ **fascinating, fascinated**

a	add	ô	order	th	this
ā	ace	o͞o	took	zh	vision
â	care	o͞o	pool		
ä	palm	u	up		
e	end	û	burn	ə	=
ē	equal	yo͞o	fuse	a	in *above*
i	it	oi	oil	e	in *sicken*
ī	ice	ou	pout	i	in *possible*
o	odd	ng	ring	o	in *melon*
ō	open	th	thin	u	in *circus*

fas·ci·na·tion /fas ə nā shən/ *noun* The state of being fascinated. *Tamika has a fascination with constellations.*

fax /faks/ *noun* An exact copy of a letter, document, or such, sent along a telephone line using a special machine. *Fax is short for facsimile.*

fier·y /fī ə rē/ *adjective* 1. Like fire, or to do with fire. 2. Very emotional, as in *a fiery speech.*

first-rate /fûrst rāt/ *adjective* Excellent. *This diner makes first-rate sandwiches.*

for·eign /fôr in/ *adjective* 1. To do with, or coming from, another country. 2. Strange or unfamiliar. *That subject is foreign to me.*

for·ev·er /fôr ev ər/ *adverb* 1. For all time. *No one can expect to live forever.* 2. Always or continually. *Kent is forever asking questions.*

form /fôrm/ 1. *noun* Type or kind. 2. *noun* Shape. 3. *noun* A piece of paper with questions to be filled in. 4. *verb* To make or to organize. *We formed a rollerskating club.*

for·mal /fôr məl/ *adjective* 1. Proper and not casual. 2. Official.

for·mal·i·ty /fôr mal i tē/ *noun* Ceremony; an established form or procedure that is required or conventional.

for·mat /fôr mat/ 1. *noun* The shape or style of something. *The new magazine has a bolder format than the old one.* 2. *verb* To prepare a computer disk for writing and reading.

form·less /fôrm lis/ *adjective* Lacking a definite or regular form or shape; shapeless.

for·mu·la /fôr myə lə/ *noun* 1. A rule in science or math that is written with numbers and symbols. 2. A recipe. 3. A set of actions that will lead to a result, as in *formula for success.* 4. A liquid substitute for mother's milk.

freeze-dried /frēz drīd/ *verb* Preserved food by freezing it and then removing its moisture content in a high vacuum.

G g

ge·o·graph·i·cal /jē ə graf i kəl/ *adjective* Of, relating to, or according to geography.

ge·og·ra·phy /jē og rə fē/ *noun* The study of the earth, including its people, resources, climate, and physical features.

ge·o·log·i·cal /jē ə loj i kəl/ *adjective* Of or relating to geology.

ge·ol·o·gist /jē ol ə jist/ *noun* A scientist who studies geology.

ge·ol·o·gy /jē ol ə jē/ *noun* The study of the earth's physical history and structure.

ge·o·met·ric /jē ə me trik/ *adjective* Of or relating to geometry.

ge·om·e·try /jē om i trē/ *noun* The branch of mathematics that deals with lines, angles, shapes, and so on.

gla·cier /glā shər/ *noun* A huge mass of ice, found in mountain valleys or polar regions, that is formed when snow falls and does not melt because the temperature remains below freezing.

grace /grās/ *noun* 1. An elegant way of moving. 2. Pleasant behavior. 3. A short prayer of thanks before a meal.

grace·ful /grās fəl/ *adjective* Showing grace, especially in movement.

grand·par·ent /gran pâr ənt/ *noun* The parent of a parent.

H h

hair·cut /hâr kut/ *noun* 1. An act or instance of cutting the hair. 2. The style in which someone's hair is worn.

half-mast /haf mast/ *noun*
The position halfway between the top and bottom of a flagpole or mast. Flags are flown in this position as a sign of respect for someone who has just died.

hall·way /hôl wā/ *noun*
A corridor or passageway in a building.

hand-me-down
/hand mē doun/ *noun*
An article of clothing or another item passed along for someone else's use.

hang·ar /hang ər/ *noun*
A large building where aircraft are kept. **Hangar** sounds like **hanger**.

hang·er /hang ər/ *noun*
A piece of specially shaped wood, metal, or plastic used for hanging clothes. **Hanger** sounds like **hangar**.

he'd /hēd/ *contraction*
1. A short form of *he had* or *he would*.

her·oes /hēr ōs/ *noun, plural*
1. Brave or good people. 2. The main characters in a book, play, movie, or any kind of story.

hi·ber·nate /hī bər nāt/ *verb*
To spend the winter sleeping, as some animals do, to survive low temperatures and a lack of food.
▶ **hibernating, hibernated**

Word History

The English word **hibernate** comes from the Latin word *hibernus*, meaning "wintry." Winter is the time when certain kinds of animals hibernate.

hi·ber·na·tion
/hī bər nā shən/ *noun*
The act of hibernating.

home·room /hōm room/
noun A classroom in which students meet with their teacher before studying begins.

home run /hōm run/ *noun*
In baseball, a hit that allows the batter to run all the way around the bases and score a run.

hun·dredth /hun dridth/ *noun*
1. One part of something that has been divided into 100 equal parts, written 1/100. 2. In decimal notation, the position of the second number to the right of the decimal point, known as *the hundredths place*. In the number 4.0129, the digit 1 is in the hundredths place.

hys·ter·i·cal /hi ster i kəl/
adjective Very emotional; so excited or upset that a person may laugh or cry.

I i

ice cream /īs crēm/ *noun*
A sweet, frozen dessert made from milk products, various flavors, and sweeteners.

I'd /īd/ *contraction*
A short form of *I would, I had*, or *I should*.

il·lus·trate /il ə strāt/ *verb*
1. To draw pictures for a publication. 2. To make clear or explain by using examples or comparisons.

il·lus·tra·tion /il ə strā shən/
noun 1. A picture in a book, magazine, or such. 2. An example.

im·age /im ij/ *noun*
1. A picture you have in your mind. 2. A representation, such as a picture or a statue. 3. The way someone appears to other people. 4. A picture formed in a lens or a mirror.

im·ag·i·nar·y /i maj ə ner ē/
adjective Existing in the imagination and not in the real world.

a	add	ô	order	th	this
ā	ace	ōō	took	zh	vision
â	care	ōō	pool		
ä	palm	u	up		
e	end	û	burn	ə	=
ē	equal	yōō	fuse	a	in *above*
i	it	oi	oil	e	in *sicken*
ī	ice	ou	pout	i	in *possible*
o	odd	ng	ring	o	in *melon*
ō	open	th	thin	u	in *circus*

im·ag·i·na·tion
/i maj ə nā shən/ *noun*
1. The ability to form pictures in your mind of things that are not present or real. 2. Creative ability.

im·ag·i·na·tive
/i maj ə nə tiv/ *adjective*
Creative; showing imagination.

im·ag·ine /i maj in/ *verb*
To picture something in your mind. ▶ **imagining, imagined**

im·mi·gra·tion
/im ə grā shən/ *noun*
The process of coming to a new country to stay permanently.

im·por·ta·tion
/im pôr tā shən/ *noun*
The process of bringing goods into a place or country from elsewhere.

im·pos·si·bil·i·ty
/im pos ə bil i tē/ *noun*
A condition that cannot be achieved, or something that cannot be true. *Counting all the stars in the universe is an impossibility.*

im·pos·si·ble /im pos ə bəl/
adjective Not capable of occurring or existing.

im·press /im pres/ *verb*
1. To make people think highly of you. 2. To have an effect on someone's mind.

im·pres·sion /im presh ən/
noun 1. An idea or a feeling. *Raoul had the impression that Keith hadn't really read the book.* 2. An imitation of someone. *The audience laughed when the speaker changed his voice to do an impression of the President.* 3. A marked effect or influence. *The generosity of the exchange student left a strong impression on us.*

im·pro·vise /im prə vīz/ *verb*
1. To do the best you can with what is available. 2. To compose on the spur of the moment.
▶ **improvising, improvised**

in·clude /in klo̅o̅d/ *verb*
To contain something or someone as part of something else.
▶ **including, included**

in·clu·sion /in klo̅o̅ zhən/ *noun*
1. The state of being included. 2. Something that is included.

in·fec·tion /in fek shən/ *noun*
An illness caused by germs or viruses.

in·fec·tious /in fek shəs/
adjective 1. Caused or spread by germs or viruses. 2. Easily spread. *Laughter is often infectious.*

in·fo·mer·cial (information + commercial) /in fō mûr shəl/
noun A program-length television commercial with demonstrations, interviews, and detailed information about a service or product.

in·form /in fôrm/ *verb*
1. To tell someone something.
2. To give information to.
▶ **informing, informed**
Synonym: notify

in·for·mal /in fôr məl/
adjective Relaxed and casual.

in·for·mal·ly /in fôr məl ē/
adverb In a relaxed and casual way. *Yoko liked to entertain informally.*

in·for·ma·tion
/in fər mā shən/ *noun*
Facts and knowledge; facts about a specific subject or event.

in·for·ma·tion·al
/in fər mā shən əl/ *adjective*
Of or giving information. *The fire department held an informational meeting about fire safety.*

in·form·a·tive /in fôr mə tiv/
adjective Providing useful information.
Synonym: instructive

in·hale /in hāl/ *verb*
To breathe in. ▶ **inhaling, inhaled**

in·hib·it /in hib it/ *verb*
To prevent or restrain someone from doing something.

in·sen·si·tiv·i·ty
/in sen sə tiv i tē/ *noun*
The quality of being tactless or unsympathetic to other people's feelings.

in·stinct /in stingkt/ *noun*
1. Natural rather than learned behavior. 2. Knowledge or feeling without being told. *I had an instinct she was not telling the truth.*

in·te·ri·or /in tēr ē ər/
1. *noun* The inside of something, especially a building. 2. *adjective* Situated, or being within or inside.

in·ter·mis·sion
/in tər mish ən/ *noun*
A short break in activity, especially between acts of a play or a concert.

in·ter·mit·tent /in tər mit nt/
adjective Stopping and starting again; not continuous.

in·ter·nal /in tûr nl/ *adjective*
Happening or existing inside someone or something; inner.

In·ter·net /in tər net/ *noun*
A large computer network that links smaller computer networks throughout the world. *Internet is short for International network.*

in·ter·rupt /in tə rupt/ *verb*
1. To stop for a short time. 2. To start talking before someone else has finished talking.
from Latin: inter- between + *rumpere* to break

in·ter·view /in tər vyōō/ *noun*
A meeting at which someone is asked questions, as in *a job interview* or *a radio interview.*

in·tro·duce /in trə dōōs/ *verb*
1. To bring in something new.
2. To cause to be known by name.
3. To start.
from Latin: intro- in + *ducere* to lead

in·tro·duc·ing
/in trə dōōs ing/ *verb*
Bringing in or establishing something unfamiliar.

in·tro·duc·tion
/in trə duk shən/ *noun*
1. The first experience of something. 2. The act of introducing one person to another. 3. The opening words of a book, speech, and so on.

in·tro·duc·to·ry
/in trə duk tə rē/ *adjective*
Serving to introduce; of or relating to a first step.

in·var·i·a·bly
/in var ē ə blē/ *adverb*
Remaining the same or unchanged; constantly.

in·vis·i·ble /in viz ə bəl/
adjective Cannot be seen.

iss·ue /ish ōō/
1. *noun* The main topic for debate or decision. *What issues will be covered at the meeting?* 2. *noun* An edition of a newspaper or magazine. 3. *verb* To send out or give out. *The school will issue equipment to the team.* 4. *verb* To come out of. *We heard laughter issue from behind the door.*

L l

la·ser /lā zər/ *noun*
A device that makes a narrow and powerful beam of light that can be used for light shows, for cutting things, or for medical operations. *Laser stands for Light Amplification by Stimulated Emission of Radiation.*

let's /lets/ *contraction*
A short form of *let us.*

light-year /līt yēr/ *noun*
A unit for measuring distance in space. A light-year is the distance that light travels in one year.

lo·cal /lō kəl/
1. *adjective* Having to do with a certain place; near the town or neighborhood where you live.
2. *adjective* Affecting only part of the body, as in *a local anesthetic.*
3. *noun* A train, subway, or bus that makes all the stops on a route. *from Latin: locus* place

lo·cal·ly /lō kəl lē/ *adverb*
To be found near the town or neighborhood where you live.

a	add	ô	order	th	this
ā	ace	ōō	took	zh	vision
â	care	ōō	pool		
ä	palm	u	up		
e	end	û	burn	ə	=
ē	equal	yōō	fuse	a	in *above*
i	it	oi	oil	e	in *sicken*
ī	ice	ou	pout	i	in *possible*
o	odd	ng	ring	o	in *melon*
ō	open	th	thin	u	in *circus*

lo·cate /lō kāt/ *verb*
1. To find out where something is.
2. To put or place somewhere.
3. To settle in a particular place.
from Latin: locus place

lo·ca·tion /lō kā shən/ *noun*
1. The place or position where something is. 2. A place used to film a movie or TV program. *The film about the Alamo was shot on location in San Antonio.*

lock·er room /lok ər rŏŏm/ *noun* A room with lockers in a school or gym used for storing personal belongings.

lus·ter /lus tər/ *noun*
A bright shine or glow of soft, reflected light.

lynx /lingks/ *noun*
A wildcat with a short tail, light brown or orange fur, and tufts of hair on its ears.
plural **lynx** or **lynxes**

M m

man·u·fac·ture
/man yə fak chər/ *verb*
1. To make something, often with machines. 2. To invent or make something up.
from Latin: manus hand + facere to make

man·u·fac·tur·er
/man yə fak chər ər/ *noun*
A person or company who is in the business of manufacturing; especially a factory owner.

Mas·sa·chu·setts
/mas ə chŏŏ sits/ *noun*
A state in the northeast United States on the Atlantic coast.

me·chan·ic /mə kan ik/ *noun*
A person who is skilled at operating or repairing machines.

me·chan·i·cal /mə kan i kəl/
adjective 1. To do with machines or tools. 2. Operated by machinery.
3. Acting or done as if by machine, without thought or feeling.

me·di·a /mē dē ə/ *noun*
1. A plural of **medium**. 2. The means of communication, such as newspapers, magazines, television, and radio, with wide reach and influence.

meld (melt + weld) /meld/
verb To merge; to blend.

me·men·to /mə men tō/ *noun*
A small item kept to remember a place, an experience, or a person.

mem·o /mem ō/ *noun*
Short for **memorandum**: a short note designating something to be remembered.

mem·oir /mem wär/ *noun*
A narrative composed from personal experience; autobiography.

mem·o·ra·bil·i·a
/mem ər ə bil ē ə/ *noun*
1. Things that are worthy of remembering; also the things that are a record of such memories; mementos.

mem·o·ra·ble
/mem ər ə bəl/ *adjective*
Easily remembered or worth remembering.

me·mo·ri·al /mə môr ē əl/
1. *noun* Something that is built or done to help people remember a person or an event. 2. *adjective* Serving to honor a person or an event, as in *a memorial service.*

mem·o·rize /mem ə rīz/ *verb*
To learn something by heart.
▶ **memorizing, memorized**

mem·o·ry /mem ə rē/ *noun*
1. The power to remember things.
2. Something that you remember from the past. 3. Honor and respect for someone or something in the past.
from Latin: memor memory

mis·in·form /mis in fôrm/ *verb*
To give false or misleading information to.

mis·in·for·ma·tion
/mis in fər mā shən/ *noun*
False or misleading information.

mis·sile /mis əl/ *noun*
A weapon that is thrown or shot at a target.
from Latin: mittere to send

mis·sion /mish ən/ *noun*
1. A special job or task. 2. A group of people who are sent to do a special job, as in *a rescue mission*.
3. A church or other place where missionaries live and work.
from Latin: mittere to send

Mis·sis·sip·pi
/mis ə sip ē/ *noun* 1. A state in the southern United States. 2. A river flowing south from Minnesota to the Gulf of Mexico.

mo·dem (modulator + demodulator) /mō dəm/ *noun*
A piece of electronic equipment used to send information between computers over telephone lines.

mon·arch /mon ərk/ *noun*
1. A ruler, such as a king or queen, who often inherits his or her position. 2. A large orange and black butterfly.

mon·ar·chy /mon ər kē/ *noun*
A country or government ruled by a monarch. *plural* **monarchies**

mo·ped /mō ped/ *noun*
A heavy bicycle with a small engine.

mor·al /môr əl/
1. *adjective* To do with right and wrong. 2. *adjective* Good and honest. 3. *noun, plural* Beliefs about what is right and wrong. *John has very high morals.* 4. *noun* The lesson taught by a story.

mor·ale /mə ral/ *noun*
The state of mind or spirit of a person or group.

mo·tel (motor + hotel) /mō tel/ *noun*
A roadside hotel with parking spaces next to the rooms.

moth·ers-in-law /muth ərs in lô/ *noun, plural*
The mothers of spouses.

mo·tor·cade (motor + cavalcade) /mō tər kād/ *noun*
A procession of motor vehicles. *Police officers surrounded the President's motorcade.*

mul·ti·pli·ca·tion /mul tə pli kā shən/ *noun*
The mathematical operation of multiplying.

mul·ti·ply /mul tə plī/ *verb*
1. To add the same number to itself several times. *If you multiply 3 times 5, you get 15.* 2. To grow in number or amount.

my·self /mī self/ *pronoun*
Me and no one else. *I have hurt myself.*

myth /mith/ *noun*
1. A story that expresses the beliefs of a group of people, tells about gods or goddesses, or tries to explain natural events. 2. A false idea that many people believe. *It is a myth that you can get warts by touching a toad.*

N n

nine·ty-five /nīn tē fīv/ *noun*
Ten times nine, plus five.

non·com·mit·tal /non kə mit l/ *adjective*
Not committing yourself to one course of action or one point of view. *When asked about her future plans, Tomoko remained noncommittal.*

no one /nō wun/ *pronoun*
Not a single person. *There was no one in the park.*

no·where /nō hwâr/
1. *adverb* Not any place. *There was nowhere to hide.* 2. *noun* An unknown or unimportant place or state of being. *The swimmer rose from nowhere to become a champion.*

a	add	ô	order	th	this
ā	ace	ōō	took	zh	vision
â	care	ōō	pool		
ä	palm	u	up		
e	end	û	burn	ə	=
ē	equal	yōō	fuse	a	in *above*
i	it	oi	oil	e	in *sicken*
ī	ice	ou	pout	i	in *possible*
o	odd	ng	ring	o	in *melon*
ō	open	th	thin	u	in *circus*

O o

ob·ser·va·tion
/ob zûr vā shən/ *noun*
1. The careful watching of someone or something.
2. Something that you have noticed by watching carefully.
3. A remark.

ob·serve /əb zurv/ *verb*
1. To watch carefully. 2. To notice something by looking or watching.
3. To make a remark.
4. To follow or to obey. 5. To celebrate.
▶ observing, observed
▶ *noun* observance

oc·cur /ə kûr/ *verb*
1. To happen. 2. To come to mind.
▶ occurring, occurred

oc·cur·rence /ə kûr əns/ *noun*
Something that occurs; an event.

o'clock /ə klok/ *adverb*
A word used when saying what the time is. *O'clock is short for "of the clock."*

old-fash·ioned
/ōld fash ənd/ *adjective*
1. No longer fashionable or popular. 2. Attached to or keeping the ways, ideas, or customs of an earlier time, as in *an old-fashioned wedding.*

o·mit /ō mit/ *verb*
To leave something out. *Hans decided to omit a line from the song.*

o·mit·ting /ō mit ing/ *verb*
Leaving something out. *Hans is omitting a line from the song.*

or·gan·ize /ôr gə nīz/ *verb*
1. To plan and run an event. 2. To arrange things neatly and in order.

our·selves /är selvz/ *pronoun*
Us and no one else. *We're proud of ourselves.*

o·ver·board /ō vər bôrd/
adverb 1. Over the side of a boat.
2. Overly enthusiastic about.

o·ver·cast /ō vər kast/
adjective Covered with clouds.

o·ver·come /ō vər kum/ *verb*
1. To defeat or deal with something. *Before learning to swim, I had to overcome my fear of water.* 2. To strongly affect, as in *overcome with emotion.*
▶ overcoming, overcame

o·ver·due /ō vər dōō/ *adjective*
Behind schedule; late.

o·ver·hear /ō vər hēr/ *verb*
To hear what someone else is saying when the person does not know that you are listening.
▶ overhearing, overheard

o·ver·joyed /ō vər joid/
adjective Extremely happy.

o·ver·lap /ō vər lap/ *verb*
To cover part of something.
▶ overlapping, overlapped

o·ver·look /ō vər look/ *verb*
1. To look down on from a higher place. 2. To fail to notice something or to choose to ignore it.

o·ver·pop·u·lat·ed
/ō vər pop yə lā təd/ *adjective*
Too large a population of humans or animals to be sustained by the natural resources available in an area.

o·ver·re·ac·tion
/ō vər rē ak shən/ *noun*
An excessive response.

o·ver·slept /ō vər slept/ *verb*
To have slept for longer than intended.

o·ver·take /ō vər tāk/ *verb*
1. To catch up with. 2. To come upon suddenly or by surprise.
▶ overtaking, overtook, overtaken

o·ver·turn /ō vər tûrn/ *verb*
1. To turn over. 2. To reverse a decision that someone else has made.

o·ver·whelmed
/ō vər hwelmd/ *verb*
1. Defeated.
2. Strongly affected.
I was overwhelmed by my work.

ox·y·gen
/ok si jən/ *noun*
A colorless gas found in the air. Humans and animals need oxygen to breathe, and fires need oxygen to burn. Oxygen makes up 21 percent of Earth's atmosphere.

P p

pa·ren·the·ses
/pə ren thə sēs/ *noun*
Plural of **parenthesis**. A pair of curved lines that enclose a word or phrase.

pas·time /pas tīm/ *noun*
A hobby, sports activity, or entertainment that makes the time pass in an enjoyable way.
Watching basketball is my favorite pastime.

pen·i·cil·lin /pen ə sil in/
noun A drug made from a mold called *penicillium* that kills bacteria and helps fight some diseases. Penicillin was the first antibiotic and was discovered in 1928.

pen·in·su·la /pə nin sə lə/
noun A piece of land that sticks out from a larger land mass and is almost completely surrounded by water. *The state of Florida is a peninsula.*

per·ceive /pər sēv/ *verb*
1. To become aware of through the senses, especially through sight and hearing. 2. To understand. *She could perceive that I was angry.*

per·cent /pər sent/ *noun*
One part in a hundred, written using the symbol %. *A quarter is 25% of one dollar.*
from Latin: centum hundred

per·cent·age /pər sen tij/
noun A fraction or a portion of something expressed as a number out of a hundred.

per·fect
1. /pûr fikt/ *adjective* Without any flaws or mistakes. 2. /pər fekt/
verb To succeed with effort at making something work well.

per·fec·tion /pər fek shən/
noun The state or quality of being without flaws.

per·mis·sion /pər mish ən/
noun Authorization granted to a person to do something.

per·mit
1. /pər mit/ *verb* To allow.
2. /pûr mit/ *noun* A written statement giving permission for something, as in a *driving permit*.
▶ *verb* permitting, permitted

per·mit·ting /pər mit ing/
verb Allowing.

phys·i·cal /fiz i kəl/ *adjective*
1. To do with the body. 2. Relating to matter and objects.

phy·si·cian /fi zish ən/ *noun*
A medical doctor.

pierce /pērs/ *verb*
1. To make a hole in something.
2. To pass into or through, as with a sharp instrument. *A coyote's cry can pierce the night.*

po·em /pō əm/ *noun*
A piece of writing set out in short lines, often with a noticeable rhythm and some words that rhyme.

po·et /pō it/ *noun*
A person who writes poetry.

po·et·ic /pō et ik/ *adjective*
Of, relating to, or like poetry.

pol·ka dot /pō kə dot/ *noun*
One of many round dots that are repeated to form a regular pattern on fabric or other materials.

pop·u·lar /pop yə lər/ *adjective*
1. Liked or enjoyed by many people. 2. Of, for, or by the people, as in *popular elections*.
from Latin: populus people

pop·u·lar·i·ty
/pop yə lar i tē/ *noun*
The quality or state of being popular.

pop·u·lar·ly /pop yə lər lē/
adverb Describing how or why someone is liked or enjoyed by many people. *She is the most popularly acclaimed actress of our time.*

pop·u·late /pop yə lāt/ *verb*
To supply with inhabitants; to live in.
from Latin: populus people

a	add	ô	order	th	this
ā	ace	o͞o	took	zh	vision
â	care	o͞o	pool		
ä	palm	u	up		
e	end	û	burn	ə	=
ē	equal	yo͞o	fuse	a	in *above*
i	it	oi	oil	e	in *sicken*
ī	ice	ou	pout	i	in *possible*
o	odd	ng	ring	o	in *melon*
ō	open	th	thin	u	in *circus*

pop·u·la·tion
/pop yə lā shən/ *noun*
1. The total number of people living in a certain place. 2. All of the people living in a certain place.

pos·si·ble /pos ə bəl/ *adjective*
Capable of happening, being done, or being used for a certain purpose.

po·ta·toes /pə tā tōs/ *noun*
The thick underground edible tubers of the potato plant.

pre·cede /pri sēd/ *verb*
To come before something else.
from Latin: pre- before + cedere to go

pre·sent
1. /pri zent/ *verb* To give a gift in a formal way. 2. /pri zent/ *verb* To introduce something. 3. /prez ənt/ *noun* A gift. 4. /prez ənt/ *noun* The time that is happening now. 5. /prez ənt/ *adjective* Being at hand. *I was present when Mr. Reyes took attendance.*

pres·en·ta·tion
/prez ən tā shən/ *noun*
1. The act of giving a prize or present. 2. The way that something is produced and the way it looks.

pre·view /prē vyoo/ *noun*
A showing of a play or a screening of a movie before it is released to the general public.

pro·ceed /prə sēd/ *verb*
To move forward or continue.
from Latin: pro- forward + cedere to go

pro·duce
1. /prə doos/ *verb* To make something. 2. /prə doos/ *verb* To bring forth. *The volcano started to produce lava.* 3. /prod oos/ *noun* Fresh vegetables or fruit grown for eating.
from Latin: pro- forward + ducere to lead

pro·duc·ing /prə doos ing/
verb Making something, or bringing something forth. *Noah is producing a new play.*

prod·uct /prod əkt/ *noun*
1. Something produced; a result. 2. The result you get when you multiply two numbers.
from Latin: pro- forward + ducere to lead

pro·duc·tion /prə duk shən/
noun 1. The process of manufacturing or growing something. 2. The total amount produced. 3. A play or other public entertainment that is presented to others.

pro·duc·tive /prə duk tiv/
adjective Making a lot of products or producing good results.

pro·duc·tiv·i·ty
/prō duk tiv i tē/ *noun*
The quality or state of being productive.

pro·tein /prō tēn/ *noun*
A substance found in all living plant and animal cells. Foods such as meat, cheese, eggs, beans, and fish are sources of dietary protein.

pro·vide /prə vīd/ *verb*
1. To supply something needed or useful. 2. To set down as a rule or condition.

pro·vi·sion /prə vizh ən/ *noun*
1. The act of providing something. 2. Something that is named as a condition in an agreement, a law, or a document.

pub·li·cize /pub lə sīz/ *verb*
To announce or advertise an event, and make it known to as many people as possible.

punc·tu·a·tion
/pungk choo ā shən/ *noun*
The use of periods, commas, and other marks to make the meaning of written material clear.

pyr·a·mid /pir ə mid/ *noun*
A solid shape with a polygon as a base and triangular sides that meet at a point on top.

Q q

quar·ter·back
/kwôr tər bak/ *noun*
In football, the player who leads the offense by passing the ball or handing it off to a runner.

quiz·zes /kwiz iz/
1. *noun* Short tests. 2. *verb*
Questions someone closely.
▶ *verb* quizzing, quizzed

R r

ra·dar /rā där/ *noun*
A device for finding the location
of solid objects by reflecting radio
waves off them and receiving the
reflected waves. *Radar* stands for
RAdio Detecting And Ranging.

ra·tios /rā shē ōs/ *noun*
The comparisons between two
sets of numbers by using division.
Ratios are usually expressed as
fractions or by using the word "to."

re·act /rē akt/ *verb*
1. To respond to something that
happens. 2. To undergo a
chemical reaction.

re·ac·tion /rē ak shən/ *noun*
An action in response to
something.

re·al·ize /rē ə līz/ *verb*
1. To become aware that
something is true. 2. To make real
or to achieve. *Monique realized
her dream of climbing a mountain.*

re·ceipt /ri sēt/ *noun*
A piece of paper showing that
money, goods, mail, or a service
has been received.

re·ceiv·er /ri sē vər/ *noun*
1. Someone or something that
receives. 2. An electronic device
that receives radio or television
signals and converts them into
sounds and pictures. 3. The part
of a telephone that you hold in
your hand.
from Latin: re- back + *capere* to
take

re·cent /rē sənt/ *adjective*
Happening, made, or done a
short time ago.

rec·og·nize /rek əg nīz/ *verb*
1. To see someone and know who
the person is. 2. To understand a
situation and accept it as true.

rec·re·a·tion /rek rē ā shən/
noun The games, sports, hobbies,
and such that people enjoy in
their spare time.

rec·re·a·tion·al
/rek rē ā shən əl/ *adjective*
Of or relating to recreation.

re·duce
/ri dōōs/ or /ri dyōōs/ *verb*
To make something smaller or less.
from Latin: re- back + *ducere* to
lead

re·duc·ing
/ri dōōs ing/ or /ri dyōōs ing/
verb Making something smaller or
less.

re·duc·tion /ri duk shən/ *noun*
1. The act or process of reducing.
2. The amount by which
something is reduced.

re·form /ri fôrm/
1. *verb* To make or become better
by correcting faults. 2. *noun* An
improvement, or the correcting of
something unsatisfactory, as in
health reform.

re·form·ing /ri fôrm ing/ *verb*
Making something or someone
better by correcting faults.

re·late /ri lāt/ *verb*
1. To narrate, or tell the story of.
2. To connect in some way. *All
the questions on the quiz relate to
ancient Greece.*
3. To get along well together or
understand each other.

re·la·tion /ri lā shən/ *noun*
1. A connection between two or
more things. 2. A member of your
family.

re·lax /ri laks/ *verb*
1. To rest and take things easy.
2. To become less tense and
anxious. 3. To make less strict.

re·lax·a·tion /rē lak sā shən/
noun The act
of relaxing or
the state of
being relaxed.

a	add	ô	order	th	this
ā	ace	o͞o	took	zh	vision
â	care	o͞o	pool		
ä	palm	u	up		
e	end	û	burn	ə	=
ē	equal	yo͞o	fuse	a	in *above*
i	it	oi	oil	e	in *sicken*
ī	ice	ou	pout	i	in *possible*
o	odd	ng	ring	o	in *melon*
ō	open	th	thin	u	in *circus*

re·lieve /ri lēv/ *verb*
1. To ease someone's trouble or pain. 2. To take over someone's job or duty. *Jay will relieve Althea on lifeguard duty at noon.*

re·lo·cate /rē lō kāt/ *verb*
To move to a new place.
from Latin: re- again + locare to place

re·mem·ber /ri mem bər/ *verb*
1. To recall or bring back to mind. 2. To keep in mind carefully. *Remember to buy some milk at the store.*
from Latin: re- back, again + mentis mind

re·mem·brance
/ri mem brəns/ *noun*
1. The act or state of remembering. 2. The ability to remember. 3. A memory.
4. Something that serves to keep or bring to mind; memento.

re·sent /ri zent/ *verb*
To feel hurt or angry about something.

res·er·va·tion
/rez ər vā shən/ *noun*
1. An arrangement to save space or a seat for someone. 2. An area of land set aside by the government for a special purpose. 3. Something that causes doubt. *I have reservations about trusting him.*

re·serve /ri zûrv/
1. *verb* To save or set aside for later use. 2. *verb* To keep for oneself. *The defendant reserves the right to remain silent.* 3. *noun* A supply of something saved for later use.

res·o·lu·tion /rez ə lōo shən/
noun 1. A promise to yourself that you will try hard to do something, as in *New Year's resolutions.*
2. The state of being very determined.

re·solve /ri zolv/ *verb*
1. To make a firm decision. *Stacey resolved to learn another language.*
2. To deal with a problem successfully. ▶ **resolving, resolved**

re·spect /ri spekt/
1. *verb* To admire and have a high opinion of someone; to look up to. 2. *noun* A feeling of admiration and regard. 3. *noun* A detail or particular part of something. *In many respects, Guy's plan is a good one.*
from Latin: re- back + specere to look

re·spect·ful /ri spekt fəl/
adjective Showing respect; courteous.

re·un·ion /rē yōon yən/ *noun*
A meeting between people who have not seen each other for a long time, as in *a family reunion.*
from Latin: re- again + unus one

re·vise /ri vīz/ *verb*
To look over again and change or correct; to update. ▶ **revised, revising**
from Latin: re- again + videre to see

re·vi·sion /ri vizh ən/ *noun*
1. The act of revising. 2. A change or alteration.

rhyme /rīm/
1. *verb* To sound the same. *The word* seat *rhymes with* beat. 2. *verb* To use words that end with the same sounds. 3. *noun* A short poem.

rhythm /riṫh əm/ *noun*
A regular beat in poetry, music, or dance.

run·ner-up /run ər up/ *noun*
The person or team who comes in second in a race or competition.

S s

sat·is·fac·tion
/sat is fak shən/ *noun*
The state of being satisfied; contentment.

sat·is·fact·o·ry
/sat is fak tə rē/ *adjective*
Good enough but not outstanding.

sche·dule /skej ōol/
1. *noun* A plan, program, or timetable. 2. *verb* To plan an event for a particular time.

scu·ba /skōo bə/ *noun*
Portable equipment used by divers for breathing underwater. *Scuba stands for Self-Contained Underwater Breathing Apparatus.*

sec·ond-rate /sek ənd rāt/
adjective Not very good, as in *second-rate merchandise.*

seize /sēz/ *verb*
1. To grab or take hold of something suddenly. 2. To arrest or capture someone or something.

self-con·trol /self kən trōl/
noun Control of your feelings or
behavior. *The boy showed great
self-control during the long lecture.*
▶ *adjective* self-controlled

self-de·fense /self di fens/
noun The act of protecting
yourself against attacks or threats.

sense /sens/ *noun*
1. One of the powers a living
being uses to learn about its
surroundings. Sight, hearing,
taste, touch, and smell are the five
senses. 2. *noun* A feeling, as in *a
sense of security.* 3. *noun* Good
judgment. 4. *noun* Meaning.
5. *verb* To feel or be aware of
something. *I sensed someone
standing over my desk.*
from Latin: sentire to feel, to
perceive

sen·si·tive /sen si tiv/ *adjective*
1. Easily hurt or upset. 2. Aware
of people's feelings. 3. Able to
react to the slightest change.
4. Painful.
from Latin: sentire to feel, to
perceive

sen·si·tiv·i·ty /sen si tiv i tē/
noun 1. The state of being
sensitive. 2. The ability to respond
to stimulation.
from Latin: sentire to feel, to
perceive

se·ri·al /sēr ē əl/ *noun*
A story that is told in several
parts. The parts are presented one
at a time in a magazine or on
television or radio.

ser·ies /sēr ēz/ *noun*
1. A group of related things that
follow in order. 2. A number of
television or radio programs or
books that are linked in some
way.

she'd /shēd/ *contraction*
A short form of *she had* or *she
would.*

sher·iffs /sher ifs/ *noun*
People in charge of enforcing the
law in a county.

side ef·fect /sīd i fekt/ *noun*
A usually negative effect of taking
a medicine besides the intended
effect.

sign lan·guage
/sīn lang gwij/ *noun*
A language in which hand
gestures, in combination with
facial expressions and larger body
movements, are used instead of
speech.

sim·i·lar /sim ə lər/ *adjective*
Alike, but not exactly the same.

sim·i·lar·i·ty /sim ə lar i tē/
noun 1. The state of being similar.
2. A likeness or resemblance.

sim·pli·fi·ca·tion
/sim plə fi kā shən/ *noun*
1. The act or process of
simplifying. 2. A result of
simplifying.

sim·pli·fy /sim plə fī/ *verb*
To make easier or less
complicated.
▶ simplifying, simplified, simplifies

sin·gle-han·ded
/sing gəl han did/ *adjective*
Done alone or without help from
others.

sit·com /sit kom/ *noun*
A humorous television program
that features the same group of
characters each week. *Sitcom* is
short for *situation comedy.*

skied /skēd/ *verb*
To have traveled on long slender
runners over water or snow.

ski·ing /skē ing/ *verb* The act
of traveling on long slender
runners over water or snow.

sky·scrap·er /skī skrā pər/
noun A very tall building.

sleep·ing bag /slē ping bag/
noun A padded bag used for
sleeping, especially when
camping.

slosh (slop + slush) /slosh/
verb To splash through water,
mud, or slush.

a	add	ô	order	th	this
ā	ace	o͞o	took	zh	vision
â	care	o͞o	pool		
ä	palm	u	up		
e	end	û	burn	ə	=
ē	equal	yo͞o	fuse	a	in *above*
i	it	oi	oil	e	in *sicken*
ī	ice	ou	pout	i	in *possible*
o	odd	ng	ring	o	in *melon*
ō	open	th	thin	u	in *circus*

smash (smack + mash)
/smash/
1. *verb* To break or crush; to collide. 2. *verb* To destroy or defeat completely. 3. *noun* The act or sound of smashing. 4. *noun* A recording, movie, or show that is very successful.

smog (smoke + fog) /smog/
noun Polluted air that is a mixture of fog and smoke.

soc·cer /sok ər/
noun A game played by two 11-player teams who try to score by kicking a ball into goals at each end of a field.

so·cia·ble /sō shə bəl/ *adjective*
To be friendly and enjoy spending time with other people.

so·cial /sō shəl/
1. *adjective* Relating to the way people live together as a society. 2. *adjective* Having to do with people getting together in a friendly way. 3. *adjective* Friendly; enjoying company. 4. *noun* A gathering or party.
from Latin: socius companion

soc·ial·ly /sō shəl ē/ *adverb*
Describing how something does or does not relate to the way people live together in a society. *Talking in a theater is socially unacceptable.*

so·ci·e·ty /sə sī i tē/ *noun*
1. All people, or people as a group. 2. An organization for people who share the same interests.
from Latin: socius companion

so·lar en·er·gy
/sō lər en ər jē/ *noun*
Energy from the sun that can be used for heating and generating electricity.

so·lar sys·tem
/sō lər sis təm/ *noun*
The sun and the bodies that move in orbit around it. In our solar system there are nine planets, many moons, and also asteroids and comets.

sol·emn /sol əm/ *adjective*
Grave or very serious.

so·los /sō lōz/ *noun*
Pieces of music that are played or sung by one person, with or without accompaniment.

so·lu·tion /sə loo shən/ *noun*
1. The answer to a problem; an explanation. 2. A mixture formed by dissolving a substance in a liquid.

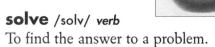

solve /solv/ *verb*
To find the answer to a problem.

some·bod·y /sum bod ē/
1. *pronoun* A person who is not specified or known. 2. *noun* An important or famous person. *When I grow up, I'm going to be somebody.*

some·thing /sum thing/
1. *pronoun* A thing that is not specified or known. *You should take something for that cold.* 2. *adverb* A little bit. *Bernardo looks something like my brother.*

spe·cies /spē shēz/ or /spē sēz/ *noun* One of the groups into which animals and plants of the same genus are divided according to their shared characteristics. *Lions, tigers, and leopards belong to the same species.*

splat·ter (splash + spatter)
/splat ər/ *verb*
To splash with drops.
▶ *verb* splattering, splattered
▶ *noun* splatter

spring·time /spring tīm/ *noun*
1. The season of spring. 2. The first or earliest period.

squig·gle (squirm + wriggle)
/skwig əl/ *verb*
1. To squirm, wriggle. 2. To write hastily, scribble.

squinch (squint + pinch)
/skwinch/ *verb*
To squeeze together or make smaller.

star·board /stär bôrd/
1. *noun* The right-hand side of a ship or an aircraft. 2. *adjective* On or toward the starboard.

star·dust /stär dust/ *noun*
1. A cluster of stars too distant to be seen individually with the naked eye. 2. A dreamlike quality.

star·fish /stär fish/ *noun*
A sea animal with five or more arms. A starfish is shaped like a star.

star·gaz·er /stär gā zer/ *noun* 1. A person who watches the stars; an astronomer. 2. A daydreamer.

star·less /stär lis/ *adjective*
Without stars; with no stars visible.

star·light /stär līt/ *noun*
The light given by the stars at night.

star·ry-eyed /stär ē īd/ *adjective* Impractical; idealistic.

star-span·gled /stär spang gəld/ *adjective* Decorated with stars.

star-stud·ded /stär stud əd/ *adjective* Lighted by or full of stars.

stel·lar /stel ər/ *adjective*
1. Of or relating to stars.
2. Excellent; outstanding. *Alice gave a stellar performance in the school play.*

ster·e·os /ster ē ōs/ *noun*
Phonographs, radios, or other sound systems that use two or more channels of sound so the listener hears sound in a more natural way.

sub·di·vi·sion /sub di vizh ən/ *noun*
1. A smaller part of something that has already been divided. 2. An area of land divided into lots for homes.

sub·ject /sub jikt/ *noun*
1. The person or thing that is discussed or thought about in a book, newspaper article, talk, and so on. 2. An area of study.
3. /səb jekt/ *verb* To cause to experience. *Our neighbors subjected us to loud music all night.* ▶ subjecting, subjected

sub·ma·rine /sub mə rēn/
1. *noun* A ship that can travel both on the surface of and under the water. 2. *adjective* Situated or living under the surface of the sea.

sub·merge /səb mûrj/ *verb*
1. To sink beneath the surface of a liquid. 2. To cover with water or another liquid.

sub·mit /səb mit/ *verb*
1. To hand in or put something forward. 2. To agree to obey; to give in; yield. *I had to submit to my mother's wishes.*
from Latin: sub- under + mittere to send

sub·or·di·nate /sə bôr dn it/
1. *adjective* Less important; lower in rank. 2. *noun* Someone who is lower in rank or importance.

sub·sti·tute /sub sti toot/
1. *noun* Something or someone used in place of another. 2. *verb* To put or use in place of another.

sub·ter·ran·ean /sub tə rā nē ən/ *adjective*
Lying beneath the surface of the earth; underground.
from Latin: sub- under + terra earth

sub·tract /səb trakt/ *verb*
To take one number away from another.

sub·tro·pics /sub trop iks/ *noun* Regions on the earth that border the tropical zone.

sub·urb /sub ûrb/ *noun*
An area or district that is outside of but close to a city.
from Latin: sub- under, near + urbs city

sub·ur·ban /sə bûr bən/ *adjective* Of, relating to, characteristic of, or located in a suburb.

sub·way /sub wā/ *noun*
A train or a system of trains that runs underground in a city.

sub·ze·ro /sub zēr ō/ *adjective*
Indicating lower than zero degrees on a temperature scale.

sum·mar·ize /sum ə rīz/ *verb*
To state the main points of.

sum·mer·time /sum ər tīm/ *noun* The season of summer.

a	add	ô	order	th	this
ā	ace	ŏŏ	took	zh	vision
â	care	ōō	pool		
ä	palm	u	up		
e	end	û	burn	ə	=
ē	equal	yōō	fuse	a	in *above*
i	it	oi	oil	e	in *sicken*
ī	ice	ou	pout	i	in *possible*
o	odd	ng	ring	o	in *melon*
ō	open	th	thin	u	in *circus*

su·per·fic·ial /soo̅ pər fish əl/
adjective **1.** On the surface, as in *a superficial cut.* **2.** Not deep or not thorough. *The news story gave a superficial account of the event.*

su·per·hu·man
/soo̅ pər **hyoo̅** mən/ *adjective*
Having or requiring abilities beyond those of an ordinary human. *Lifting a car would require superhuman strength.*

su·per·im·pose
/soo̅ pər im **pōz**/ *verb*
To lay on top of something else; to add. ▶ **superimposing, superimposed**

su·per·in·ten·dent
/soo̅ pər in **ten** dənt/ *noun*
1. An official who directs or manages an organization, as in *superintendent of schools.* **2.** A person in charge of a building.

su·pe·ri·or /sə **pēr** ē ər/
1. *adjective* Higher in rank or position, as in *a superior officer.* **2.** *adjective* Above average in quality or ability. **3.** *noun* A person who has a higher rank or position than others.

su·per·la·tive /sə **pûr** lə tiv/
adjective **1.** Of the highest kind or order. **2.** Designating the highest degree of comparison of adjectives and adverbs: *Best* is the superlative of *good.*

su·per·mar·ket
/soo̅ pər **mär** kit/ *noun*
A large store that sells food and household items.

su·per·pow·er
/soo̅ pər **pou** ər/ *noun*
A nation with political power over other powerful nations. *The United States became a superpower after World War II.*

su·per·son·ic
/soo̅ pər **son** ik/ *adjective*
Faster than the speed of sound.

su·per·vise /soo̅ pər **vīz**/ *verb*
To watch over or direct a group of people.
from Latin: super- over *+ videre* to see
▶ **supervising, supervised**

syl·la·ble /**sil** ə bəl/ *noun*
A unit of sound in a word.

sym·bol /**sim** bəl/ *noun*
A design or an object that stands for or represents something else. **Symbol** sounds like **cymbal.**

sym·met·ri·cal /si **me** tri kəl/
adjective Having matching points, parts, or shapes on both sides of a dividing line. The capital letters *M* and *X* are symmetrical because you can draw a line dividing them into two matching halves.

sym·pa·thize /**sim** pə thīz/
verb **1.** To understand or appreciate other people's troubles. **2.** To be in agreement. *We sympathize with your views.*

sym·pa·thy /**sim** pə thē/ *noun*
1. The understanding and sharing of other people's troubles. **2.** The harmony of feeling existing between persons of like opinions.

sym·pho·ny /**sim** fə nē/ *noun*
1. A long piece of music for an orchestra. **2.** A large orchestra that usually plays classical music.
plural **symphonies**

symp·tom /**simp** təm/ *noun*
1. Something that shows that you have an illness. **2.** An indication of something.

syn·chro·nize /**sing** krə nīz/
verb To make happen at the same time or rate.
from Greek: syn- together *+ chronos* time
▶ **synchronizing, synchronized**

syn·o·nym /**sin** ə nim/ *noun*
A word that means the same or nearly the same as another word.
from Greek: syn- together *+ onoma* name

syr·up /**sir** əp/ *or* /**sûr** əp/ *noun*
1. A thick, sweet liquid made by boiling sugar and water. **2.** A sweet, thick liquid made by boiling down the sap of a tree or plant, as in *maple syrup.*

sys·tem /**sis** təm/ *noun*
1. A group of things or parts that exist or work together in an organized way. **2.** A way of organizing or arranging things.

T t

tan·ge·lo (tangerine + pomelo) /tan jə **lō**/ *noun*
A hybrid fruit that is a cross between a tangerine and a grapefruit.

tape re·cor·der
/tāp ri kôrd ər/ *noun*
A machine that you use to play
back or record music and sound
on magnetic tape.

**tax·i·cab (taximeter +
cabriolet)** /tak sē kab/ *noun*
A car that carries
passengers for a
fare.

team·mate
/tēm māt/ *noun*
A fellow member of a team.

teen·ag·er /tēn ā jər/ *noun*
A person who is between the ages
of 13 and 19.
▶ *adjective* teenage, teenaged

tel·e·thon /tel ə thon/ *noun*
A television program broadcast
over many hours, usually to raise
money for a charity or cause.

tel·e·vise /tel ə vīz/ *verb*
To broadcast by television.
▶ televising, televised

tel·e·vi·sion /tel ə vizh ən/
noun A piece of equipment with a
screen that receives and shows
moving pictures with sound.

tem·po /tem pō/ *noun*
The timing of a piece of music.

tem·po·rar·i·ly
/tem pə rer ə lē/ *adverb*
For the time being; during a
limited time.

tem·po·rar·y /tem pə rer ē/
adjective Lasting only for a time;
not permanent.

Ten·nes·see /ten ə sē/ *noun*
A state in the southeast United
States.

ter·race /ter əs/ *noun*
1. A patio, porch, or balcony. 2. A
raised, flat platform of land with
sloping sides.
from Latin: terra earth

ter·ra·cot·ta /ter ə kot ə/
noun A hard brown-red clay used
for pottery, statuettes, and
architectural purposes.

ter·rain /tə rān/ *noun*
Ground, or land, especially in
terms of its physical features, as in
rocky terrain.
from Latin: terra earth

ter·rar·i·um /tə râr ē əm/
noun A glass container for growing
small plants or raising small land
animals.
from Latin: terra earth

ter·res·tri·al /tə res trē əl/
adjective To do with the earth, or
living on the earth.
from Latin: terra earth

ter·ri·er /ter ē ər/ *noun*
Any of several breeds of small,
lively dogs.

ter·ri·tor·i·al /ter ə tôr ē əl/
adjective 1. Relating to territory.
2. Of or belonging to a specific
territory.

ter·ri·to·ry /ter i tôr ē/ *noun*
1. An area of land; a region.
2. The land and waters under the
control of a state, nation, or ruler.
from Latin: terra earth

that's /thats/ *contraction*
A short form of *that is.*

the·a·ter /thē ə tər/ *noun*
1. A building where plays or
movies are shown. 2. The work of
writing, producing, or acting in
plays.

the·at·ri·cal /thē a tri kəl/
adjective 1. Having to do with the
theater. 2. Dramatic and showy.
Rodney made a theatrical entrance.

them·selves /them selvz/
pronoun Them and no one else;
their own selves. *The children
dressed themselves.*

thieves /thēvz/ *noun, plural*
People who steal things.

time·kee·per /tīm kē pər/
noun A person or thing that
measures or records time.

time·less /tīm lis/ *adjective*
Not affected or limited by time.

time·ly /tīm lē/ *adjective*
Happening at just the right time.

time-out /tīm out/ *noun*
An interruption of play in a sports
contest.

a	add	ô	order	th	this
ā	ace	ōō	took	zh	vision
â	care	ōō	pool		
ä	palm	u	up		
e	end	û	burn	ə	=
ē	equal	yōō	fuse	a	in *above*
i	it	oi	oil	e	in *sicken*
ī	ice	ou	pout	i	in *possible*
o	odd	ng	ring	o	in *melon*
ō	open	th	thin	u	in *circus*

time·piece /tīm pēs/ *noun*
An instrument that measures and records time.

time sav·er /tīm sā vər/ *noun*
A device that lessens the time needed to do something.

time·ta·ble /tīm tā bəl/ *noun*
A printed schedule of arrival and departure times of buses, trains, planes, and such.

time·worn /tīm wôrn/
adjective
Worn or impaired by time.

tis·sue /tish ōō/ *noun*
1. Soft, thin paper used for wiping, wrapping, and so on. 2. A mass of similar cells that form a particular part of an animal or plant.

tongue /tung/ *noun*
1. The movable muscle in your mouth that is used for tasting, swallowing, and talking. 2. A language.

trans·form /trans fôrm/ *verb*
To make a great change in something.
from Latin: trans- across + *forma* form

trans·for·ma·tion
/trans fər mā shən/ *noun*
The act of transforming or the condition of being transformed. *The transformation of the empty lot into a community garden is almost complete.*

trans·mis·sion
/trans mish ən/ *noun*
1. The act or process of transmitting. 2. Something transmitted.

trans·mit /trans mit/ *verb*
1. To send or pass something from one place or person to another.
2. To send out radio or television signals.
from Latin: trans- across + *mittere* send
▶ **transmitting, transmitted**

twirl (twist + whirl) /twûrl/
verb To turn or spin around quickly.

U u

u·nan·i·mous
/yōō nan ə məs/ *adjective*
Agreed on by everyone.
from Latin: unus one + *animus* mind

un·com·mon /un kom ən/
adjective Rare or unusual; out of the ordinary.

un·der·cov·er
/un dər kuv ər/ *adjective*
In a secret or hidden way.

un·der·foot /un dər fŏŏt/
adverb 1. Under your feet. 2. In the way. *My pet puppies often play underfoot.*

un·der·ground
/un dər ground/ *adverb*
Beneath the surface of the ground. *The worm burrowed underground.*

un·der·line /un dər līn/ *verb*
1. To draw a line under. 2. To stress the importance of something. ▶ **underlining, underlined**

un·der·neath /un dər nēth/
preposition Under or below.

un·der·pass /un dər pas/
noun A road that goes underneath another road or a bridge.

un·der·pop·u·lat·ed
/un dər pop yə lā tid/ *adjective*
Too small a population of humans or animals for the number of resources available in the area.

un·der·stand /un dər stand/
verb To know what something means or how something works. *I understand Spanish.*

un·der·take /un dər tāk/ *verb*
1. To agree to do a job or task; to accept a responsibility. 2. To attempt; try. ▶ **undertaking, undertook**

un·der·wa·ter
/un dər wô tər/
1. *adjective* Located, used, or done under the surface of the water.
2. *adverb* Beneath the water, as in *to travel underwater.*

u·ni·corn /yōō ni kôrn/ *noun*
An imaginary animal that looks like a horse with one straight horn growing from its forehead.

Word History

The term **unicorn** comes from the Latin words *unum*, meaning "one," and *cornu*, meaning "horn." There were legends of these pure white beasts with one horn in many countries in ancient times, including Asian, European, and Islamic nations.

u·ni·cy·cle /yo͞o ni sī kəl/
noun A vehicle that has pedals like a bicycle but only one wheel and no handlebars.

u·ni·form /yo͞o nə fôrm/
1. *noun* A special set of clothes worn by all the members of a particular group or organization.
2. *adjective* Always the same.

un·in·formed /un in fôrmd/
adjective Not informed; not educated.

un·in·ter·est·ed
/un in tər ə stid/ *adjective*
Not interested; not personally concerned.

un·ion /yo͞on yən/ *noun*
1. An organization of workers.
2. A larger group formed by joining together two or more things or people. 3. The Union: The United States of America.

u·nique /yo͞o nēk/ *adjective*
One of a kind. *Every snowflake is unique.*

u·ni·son /yo͞o nə sən/ *noun*
A state in which all members or elements behave in the same way at the same time.
from Latin: unus one + sonus sound

u·nite /yo͞o nīt/ *verb*
To join together; to bring together to make a whole.
from Latin: unus one

u·ni·ty /yo͞o ni tē/ *noun*
1. The quality or condition of being united. 2. Agreement.

u·ni·ver·sal /yo͞o nə vûr səl/
adjective 1. Shared by everyone or everything. *Happiness and sadness are universal human emotions.*
2. Found everywhere.

u·ni·verse /yo͞o nə vûrs/ *noun*
Earth, the planets, the stars, and all things that exist in space.

u·ni·ver·si·ty
/yo͞o nə vûr si tē/ *noun*
A school for higher learning after high school, where people can study for degrees, do research, or learn a profession.
plural **universities**

un·pop·u·lar /un pop yə lər/
adjective Not liked or approved of by many people.

un·sat·is·fac·to·ry
/un sat is **fak** tə rē/ *adjective*
Not good enough to meet a certain need or standard.

un·soc·ia·ble /un sō shə bəl/
adjective To be unfriendly and not enjoy being with other people.

un·time·li·ness
/un tīm lē nəs/ *noun*
The condition of not occurring at a suitable time.

un·time·ly /un tīm lē/ *adjective*
Happening before the natural or proper time. *The untimely frost damaged many of the crops.*

up·side down /up sīd doun/
adverb With the top at the bottom. *When you turn an hourglass upside down, sand begins to fall from the upper bulb to the lower one.*

u·ti·lize /yo͞ot l īz/ *verb*
To make use of. *Solar energy utilizes the sun's power to make electricity.* ▶ **utilizing, utilized**

V v

var·i·a·ble /vâr ē ə bəl/
1. *adjective* Likely to change or be changed. 2. *noun* In mathematics, a symbol that stands for a number.

var·i·a·tion /vâr ē ā shən/
noun 1. A change from the usual.
2. Something that is slightly different from another thing of the same type. *The teacher asked us to write a variation of a fable.*

va·ri·e·ty /və rī i tē/ *noun*
1. Difference, or change. 2. A selection of different things. *The jukebox has a wide variety of music.* 3. A different type of the same thing, as in *a new variety of rose.*

var·i·ous /vâr ē əs/ *adjective*
1. Of different kinds. *This juice comes in various flavors.*
2. Several.

a	add	ô	order	ᵺ	this	
ā	ace	o͞o	took	zh	vision	
â	care	o͞o	pool			
ä	palm	u	up			
e	end	û	burn	ə	=	
ē	equal	yo͞o	fuse		ə	in *above*
i	it	oi	oil		e	in *sicken*
ī	ice	ou	pout		i	in *possible*
o	odd	ng	ring		o	in *melon*
ō	open	th	thin		u	in *circus*

var·y /vâr ē/ *verb*
1. To change or to be different.
2. To make different; give variety
to. *I like to vary my route to
school.* ▶ varying, varied

veil /vāl/ *noun*
A piece of material worn by
women as a covering for the head
or face, as in *a wedding veil.*

vic·to·ri·ous /vik tôr ē əs/
adjective 1. Having won a victory.
*The victorious team was awarded a
trophy.* 2. Of or characterized by
victory.

vic·to·ry /vik tə rē/ *noun*
A success over an opponent or
enemy in a battle or contest.

vid·e·o /vid ē ō/
1. *adjective* To do with the visual
part of a television program or
computer display. 2. *noun* The
visual part of television. 3. *noun* A
videotape recording of a movie or
television show.
from Latin: videre see

vid·e·o·cas·sette
/vid ē ō kə set/ *noun*
A plastic case that contains
videotape. It can be inserted into
a VCR and used to record or play
back movies and television
programs.

vid·e·o·tape
/vid ē ō tāp/
1. *noun* Magnetic tape on which
sound and pictures are recorded.
2. *noun* A recording on magnetic
tape. 3. *verb* The act of recording
on magnetic tape.

vi·si·bi·li·ty /viz ə bil i tē/
noun The state of being able to be
seen.

vi·si·ble /viz ə bəl/ *adjective*
Capable of being seen.
from Latin: videre see

vi·sion /vizh ən/ *noun*
1. The sense of sight. 2. A sight,
real or imagined. 3. The ability to
think ahead and plan.
from Latin: videre see

vi·sor /vī zər/ *noun*
A brim that sticks out of the front
of a cap to shade the eyes from
the sun.

vis·ta /vis tə/ *noun*
1. A view or prospect. 2. A far-
reaching mental view.

vis·u·al /vizh ōō əl/ *adjective*
1. Having to do with seeing.
2. Designed or able to be seen.

vol·ca·noes /vol kā nōz/
noun Mountains with vents
through which molten lava, ash,
cinders, and gas erupt, sometimes
violently.

W w

wave·length /wāv lengkth/
noun The distance between one
crest of a wave of light or sound
and the next.

weath·er·bea·ten
/weth ər bēt ən/ *adjective*
Something that is damaged or
worn by the weather.

web·foot·ed /web fŏŏt id/
adjective Having toes that are
connected by a web or fold of skin.

well·bal·anced
/wel bal ənsd/ *adjective*
1. Nicely or evenly balanced. 2.
Sane or sensible. *A well-balanced
person is not easily upset.*

well·be·haved /wel bi hāvd/
adjective Acting properly and with
good manners.

wher·ev·er /hwâr ev ər/
conjunction In, at, or to any place.
We'll go wherever you suggest.

win·ter·time /win tər tīm/
noun The season of winter.

would·n't /wŏŏd nt/ *contraction*
A short form of *would not.*

Y y

yield /yēld/ *verb*
1. To produce something. *The
field yielded 90 tons of potatoes.*
2. To surrender or to give in. *The
troops refused to yield the town.*